BLACK STAR RISING

BLACK STAR RISING

GARVEYISM IN THE WEST

HOLLY M. ROOSE

TEXAS TECH UNIVERSITY PRESS

This book is typeset in EB Garamond. The paper used in this book meets the minimum requirements of ANSI/NISO Z39.48-1992 (R1997). ♾
Designed by Hannah Gaskamp

Library of Congress Cataloging-in-Publication Data

Names: Roose, Holly M., 1975– author. Title: Black Star Rising: Garveyism in the West / Holly M. Roose. Other titles: Garveyism in the West. Description: Lubbock, Texas: Texas Tech University Press, [2022]. | Includes bibliographical references and index. | Summary: "An exploration of Black nationalist Marcus Garvey's influence on the diverse communities of the American West"—Provided by publisher.

Identifiers: LCCN 2021049692 (print) | LCCN 2021049693 (ebook) |

ISBN 978-1-68283-127-4 (cloth) | ISBN 978-1-68283-134-2 (ebook)

Subjects: LCSH: Garvey, Marcus, 1887–1940—Influence. | African Americans—West (U.S.)—Politics and government—20th century. | Universal Negro Improvement Association. | Black Star Line, Inc. | Black nationalism—West (U.S.)—History—20th century. | Minorities—Political activity—West (U.S.)—History—20th century. | Immigrants—Political activity—West (U.S.)—History—20th century. | African Americans—West (U.S.)—Social conditions—20th century. | West (U.S.)—Race relations—History—20th century. Classification: LCC E185.97.G3 R66 2022 (print) | LCC E185.97.G3 (ebook) | DDC 320.54092—dc23/eng/20211105

LC record available at https://lccn.loc.gov/2021049692
LC ebook record available at https://lccn.loc.gov/2021049693

Printed in the United States of America
22 23 24 25 26 27 28 29 30/ 9 8 7 6 5 4 3 2 1

Texas Tech University Press
Box 41037
Lubbock, Texas 79409-1037 USA
800.832.4042
www.ttupress.org

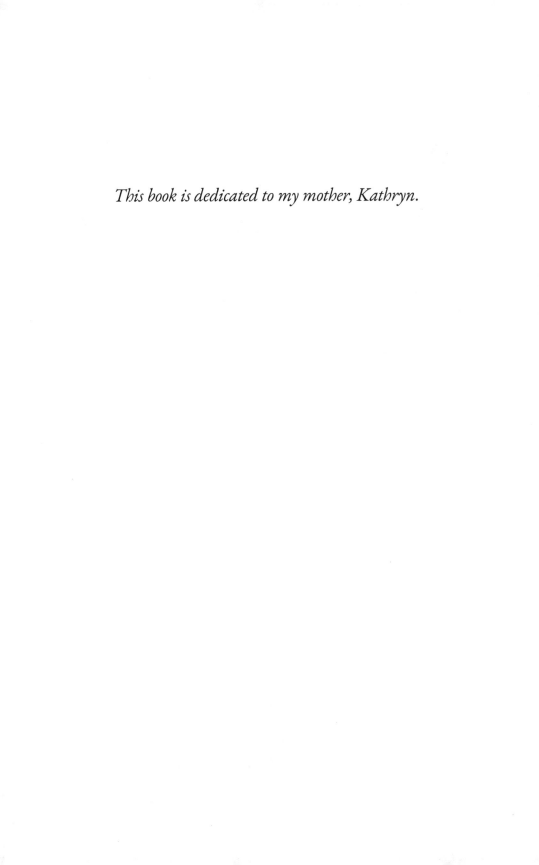

This book is dedicated to my mother, Kathryn.

CONTENTS

ACKNOWLEDGMENTS / IX

INTRODUCTION / XIII

    1   THE RETURN OF THE BLACK
        SOLDIER / 3

    2   NATIONALISMS / 35

    3   THE BLACK STAR LINE / 65

    4   THE DECLINE OF GARVEYISM
        IN THE WEST / 95

CONCLUSION / 123

NOTES / 131

BIBLIOGRAPHY / 157

INDEX / 165

ACKNOWLEDGMENTS

This was a difficult book to write, and I could not have done it without the support I received from my mentors, advisors, colleagues, students, and family. This journey began with my mentor Darrell Millner, now professor emeritus of Black Studies at Portland State University. I thought I was going to be a biology major when I finally started college at twenty-seven years of age; however, after taking just one of Darrell's courses in Black Studies, I was hooked. I switched to Black Studies and never looked back. Almost twenty years later, I'm still in love with this amazing history and Darrell is still guiding me along every step of the way. He has contributed his edits and knowledge exhaustively to multiple drafts of this work.

I would also like to thank Paul Spickard, my dissertation advisor at UC Santa Barbara, and his lovely wife, Anna, who adopted me as their own and helped me a lot since I moved to Santa Barbara. Not only did Paul maintain patience and confidence in me when I had none myself, he also nominated me for dozens of awards, talked people into giving me jobs, and edited several drafts of this book. In addition, Paul still supports me with every student emergency I bring to his doorstep while I continue my work as a teacher and mentor to low-income, underrepresented, first-generation undergraduate students. I'm forever grateful for all the delicious meals that Paul and Anna cooked for me and the trips to the cabin in Tahoe over the years. Loud dinners around the table of baked salmon, potatoes, salad, and wine will forever represent some of my best memories. I would have been utterly lost without these amazing people. Christopher McAuley, professor of Black Studies at UC Santa Barbara, was also a helpful sounding board for my ideas. I am thankful that I could run my thoughts past him as I worked out this manuscript.

In conjunction with these modern-day heroes, I'm grateful to all the people who participated in this project along the way and in the early stages. Eric Foner, one of my advisors from my days as a graduate student at Columbia University, graciously offered his time and attention to early drafts of this work. Mhoze Chikowero was quite helpful in editing portions of my chapter dealing with Africa. I'm especially thankful for the library staff at Columbia's Rare Book and Manuscripts room; the National Archives in New York City; the staff at the Schomburg in Harlem; the archival staff at the National Archives and Records Administration in Washington, DC; and the staff at the UC Santa Barbara Library. I'm extremely grateful to Ken Hough, who found information for me that I did not even know was out there. I'm also grateful to my external reviewers who took the time to make substantial comments on my manuscript.

Thank you to my colleagues in history who were helpful to my mental stability while in grad school, including Niccole Coggins, Laura Moore, Laura Hooten, and many others who have drifted in and out of my office to offer words of encouragement and support. I'm incredibly thankful to all my undergraduate students over the years. Without them, I could never have kept my sanity. They keep me balanced and always remind me of what is most important in life. I offer heartfelt thanks to Mike Miller, who, knowing nothing about me, took a chance and hired me to run his Promise Scholars program so that I can continue to work with these amazing students. I want to send a special thank you to my (at the time) high school research assistant, Natalie Torres, who is now in college herself and off to do amazing things in life.

I want to thank my family for all their support: my mother, who helped fund me when times were tough in NYC, and my sister Rajam and her husband Matt Estes for their unwavering support and encouragement and giving me a place to live when I needed it. Finally, I would like to honor all the people who have historically given (or had taken) their lives, both physically and psychologically, in the fight for global basic rights, justice, and equity.

INTRODUCTION

Between 1916 and 1925, Jamaican immigrant Marcus Garvey created in the United States what would later be recognized as the largest Black mass movement in world history. His Universal Negro Improvement Association (UNIA) is estimated to have reached an official membership of over a million by the 1920s. Hundreds of thousands of Black Americans followed and vicariously supported his organization even if they were not always dues-paying members. Established first in Jamaica in 1914 and brought to the US shortly after Garvey's arrival to Harlem in 1916, the UNIA boasted more than 700 chapters spread through thirty-eight states by the early 1920s (most US branches were in the Southern states). Internationally, there were hundreds of branches stretching across forty-one countries around the world. The publications produced by Garvey, primarily the official UNIA organ, the *Negro World*, were read and quoted around the world. Garvey's speeches had an even wider audience that stretched to the halls of power in the US national government and the imperial administrations of the European continent.

Although the early years of his life are generally known, it is worth including a brief survey here.[1] Marcus Garvey was born in 1887 in Saint Ann's Bay, Jamaica. His father was a mason, and his mother worked as a domestic and a farmworker. As a boy, Garvey served as an apprentice at a print shop and in 1909, he attempted to start his own newspaper in Jamaica titled *Garvey's Watchman,* which failed after the third issue. By 1910, Garvey began traveling around the Caribbean Basin and through Europe. Everywhere he went, typically either he would attempt to establish his own newspaper, such as his *La Nación* in Colón, Panama, or he would publish in one, such as his articles in the *African Times and Orient Review*. In 1914, after his return to Jamaica, Garvey met his first wife, Amy Ashwood, and together they founded the Universal Negro Improvement Association and African Communities League. After reading Booker T. Washington's *Up from Slavery*, Garvey envisioned a Tuskegee-like institute in Jamaica, and he began collecting funds for his organization. However, over time, his UNIA followers in Jamaica determined that he was not using their donations honestly, and his organization there began to turn against him.

Fleeing UNIA investors in Jamaica who accused him of misusing donated funds, Garvey arrived in the US in 1916, hoping to bring his relatively newly formed UNIA from Jamaica to the US—although he missed the opportunity to meet his hero Booker T. Washington, who had passed away in 1915.[2] Once in New York, he established contact with an old friend from the islands, W. A. Domingo. Born in Kingston, Jamaica, Domingo had worked in Jamaica for a brief period as a tailor's apprentice. It was during this time that Domingo and Marcus Garvey first met. Once Garvey arrived in New York, Domingo introduced his friend to a number of the important Black intellectuals of the era, among whom included Hubert Harrison and Arthur Schomburg.

In 1917, Garvey held his first UNIA meeting in Harlem with only thirteen members.[3] His friend-turned-adversary Hubert Harrison was the more popular soapbox speaker at the time. However, Garvey was soon scheduling his own lectures on the same evenings and at the same time as Harrison's. Though Harrison was more knowledgeable on global events of the day, Garvey was more animated. Recordings of Garvey's speeches still in existence reveal an incredibly charismatic speaker[4]—not unlike the later discourses of Malcolm X (whose parents were Garveyites), which would easily draw audiences into his "by any means necessary" philosophical approach to fighting racism forty years later. It was not long before Garvey's organization expanded beyond the streets of Harlem. By the mid-1920s, Garveyism existed in nearly every state in the US.

Certain features of Garveyism spoke to a universal Black[5] experience on a global scale at a time when white racism permeated all facets of government and life.[6] Black pride and the belief that Blacks had a glorious Black past that contributed to the evolution of modern civilization represented the two most important ideological components of his movement. Furthermore, the Black Star Line (BSL), a Black-owned and -operated shipping line that promised to give Blacks around the world economic autonomy, served as the most important tangible element around which Garveyites rallied.

Yet, while all Garveyites shared these basic sentiments and vision, there were significant differences in how Garveyism functioned in different locations. These differences have long been underappreciated by scholars. Regionally and globally, Garveyites altered the tenets of Garveyism in order to fit the special needs of their local circumstances. In the American South, which held more UNIA chapters than any other region or country, Garveyites organized around the separation and an accommodationist stance similar to that of Booker T. Washington in the early twentieth century. Southern UNIA chapters took these positions largely due to the harsh racial practices in the South often enforced by brutal terrorist violence— they were not able to participate in the same political and economic activities as Black people were able to do elsewhere.[7]

In the northeastern United States where Garvey himself settled, UNIA members could focus on political and economic pursuits as well as social and psychological ones. They opened businesses, such as UNIA co-op grocery stores, laundromats, tailor shops, printing presses, restaurants, and other ventures. Geographically, New York City, specifically Harlem, was the ideal location for the UNIA to organize. In Harlem, in the early twentieth century, there existed a dense network of Black radical intellectuals, including A. Philip Randolph, Hubert Harrison, Cyril Briggs, and W. A. Domingo. At the same time that Garvey was establishing his UNIA, the Harlem Renaissance and the New Negro Movement were elevating Harlem into a cosmopolitan center of racial thought and activism on the global stage. Also located there was a significant Black population, making the city a haven for Black migrants and travelers. Talented Black intellectuals, writers, artists, and musicians lived side by side and went to the same cafés and clubs. The great Black leaders and organizations of the era were also anchored in New York City, including W.E.B. DuBois and the National Association for the Advancement of Colored People (NAACP), the National Urban League, and a vibrant Black women's club movement that included figures like Madam C. J. Walker, America's first female self-made millionaire. Black business owners in New York had a critical mass of potential customers, and Black Harlemites often had more money than Blacks in other geographic regions of the country. Consequently, there was more potential for economic success and greater possibility for political power. However, with economic and political power came fierce competition between the leadership of the various Black organizations, who vied for members that could fund and otherwise support their agendas. All of the Black intellectuals mentioned here became enemies of the UNIA at some point, but Garvey's most powerful enemy was W.E.B. Du Bois and the NAACP.

Immigration was also a major component of the formation of Garveyism. The early twentieth century saw a massive influx of immigrants into the northern United States. Most emigrated from Europe, but there was another large and growing Black immigrant population in New York City as well. This Black immigrant population included at least two significant components: new arrivals from the American South and a steady influx of Black West Indians like

Garvey himself. Specifically, from 1910 to 1930, the Black population rose from 91,709 to 327,706.[8] It was this multicultural, multinational Black population that formed the foundation for Garvey's UNIA in Harlem.

By contrast, circumstances were significantly different in the American West than those of the South or the Northeast. At a time when train and boat travel through the Panama Canal were the most popular methods of getting from eastern to western US, the West was in many ways geographically isolated. At the turn of the twentieth century, California was just beginning to transition from a sparsely populated agricultural economy to a more industrialized economy. The presence of the railroads in growing cities like San Francisco and Los Angeles brought people and industry to a diversifying but still primarily agricultural region.

Twentieth-century immigrant populations in the West varied significantly from populations in the East and North. In contrast to these areas, the West had smaller infusions of European and West Indian immigrants in this period. In the West, the immigrant populations consisted primarily of populations of color from the Pacific Basin, including Pacific Islanders, mainland Chinese, Japanese, and Filipinos. In addition, the West had significant resident populations of color, including American Indigenous as well as Mexican Americans and other Central and South American immigrants. Due to the small size of the western Black population as well as the existence of these other groups of color, Garveyism on the West Coast evolved different dynamics, strategies, and objectives as compared to the eastern movement and other regions of the US. In California, Oregon, Washington, and other parts of the West, Black residents aligned with Mexican and Pacific Basin immigrants to combat the historically hostile racial environment they all faced.

Garvey scholars generally focus on his East Coast leadership, with Marcus Garvey himself as the centerpiece of analysis. Through these studies, Garvey typically falls into one of two categories of thought: he is either a great prophetic leader or a disappointing failure. The first full-length biographical sketch of Garvey took the latter approach. In his 1955 study of Garvey, *Black Moses*, E. David Cronon credits Garvey with the ability to inspire Black pride but ultimately determines that "for all his impressive organizational activities, Marcus Garvey remains a tragic, even a pathetic figure, who is today remembered more for the size of his dreams than for the practical accomplishments of his once imposing race movement."[9]

Fifteen years later, Theodore Vincent, inspired by Amy Jacques Garvey's (Marcus Garvey's second wife) *Garvey and Garveyism*, published *Black Power and the Garvey Movement* in an effort to depict Garvey and Garveyites as rational people, rather than "as dupes of a demagogue, as Cronon's book implied."[10] Vincent's work highlights the role of imperialism during and after World War I. He concludes that Garvey's movement could not have succeeded in the racial climate of the interwar years, no matter the merits of his ideas or the skill of his leadership.[11]

Tony Martin's *Race First* is another important foundational monograph on Garvey. His analysis of Garvey extends beyond the typical narrative to include Garveyism's relationship with the communists and their competition to control the agenda of Black racial activism. This was an important factor in the Garvey movement because many Garveyites turned to communism towards the 1930s. Beyond Martin's work, a number of biographies are important, including Rupert Lewis' *Marcus Garvey: Anti-Colonial Champion* and Colin Grant's *Negro with a Hat*, among others. There have also been a few geographic studies of Garveyism. Mary Rolinson's excellent work *Grassroots Garveyism* examines the Garvey movement in the American South. Rolinson provides an in-depth analysis of how Garveyism could be so successful in a region where lynching was rampant and the Klan dominated small, isolated country towns. Rolinson argues that to survive in this environment, Garveyites supported racial segregation and kept much of their organizing underground. As Rolinson explained, "They had to be more secretive than their urban associates about displays of power because their numerical superiority in the Black Belt was a more literal threat to white supremacy."[12]

The most relevant previous treatment of Garveyism in the West is that of Emory Tolbert and his book *The UNIA and Black Los Angeles*, published in 1980. Despite its brevity of only 125 pages, this work is the only book to date that examines Garveyism on the American West Coast. In addition, although it is primarily a micro study that focuses almost entirely on Los Angeles, Tolbert's study has been instrumental in terms of addressing the significant people and events of the Garveyites in that city and surrounding counties. The Los Angeles UNIA division was one of the most important on the West Coast to the parent organization in Harlem because it not only had the most members of any organization in the West but also contributed the most money to support economic ventures like the Black Star Line. When the organization split in the early twentieth century to form the Pacific Coast Negro Improvement Association, Marcus Garvey made two separate tours in an attempt to repair his most lucrative West Coast branch. For a detailed account of the Los Angeles branch, Tolbert's *UNIA in Black Los Angeles* is well worth reading.

A number of micro studies[13] and brief essays on Garveyism, which can be found in multiple academic journals, have revealed the complex nature of this short-lived movement. On the West Coast of the United States, Garveyism was not just a Black nationalist movement but a multiracial movement in which multiple nationalist groups suffering from similar oppressive circumstances found themselves at times in a common condition all along the West Coast. As a consequence, interracial organizing emerged, despite the fact that the groups were often in competition for jobs. The primary nationalist groups involved in my study are Japanese, East Asian Indian, Mexican, and Black.

None of these nationalist groups, however, can be understood or interpreted outside of the context of World War I. World War I was a European colonial war more so than a world war. Although the assassination of Archduke Franz Ferdinand of Austria-Hungary is often ascribed as the catalyst for initiating the war, the reasons for the war are contested amongst historians. The establishment of alliances among various European countries in 1914—Britain, France, and Russia on one side and Austria-Hungary, Italy, and Germany on the other—along with the competition for empire, the rise of nationalism, and the arms race, led to a war that would define the twentieth century. The war itself as well as the expansiveness and brutality of it were driven by the desire to dominate contested colonial spaces in Asia and Africa as Europeans relentlessly pursued world domination.[14]

As colonial subjects, more than a million Black West Indians, Africans, and Indians from South Asia fought for their respective colonial governments in the war. Additionally, hundreds of thousands of Black Americans were conscripted or volunteered for the war. For those who actually went to the battlefields of Europe or Africa, upon their return to their respective countries—contrary to the promises made by their national or colonial governments—the prewar white supremacist policies of the imperialist administrations had not changed, heightening the frustrations of returning veterans of color. Black nationalism throughout the Western Hemisphere and in Europe radicalized because of the unchanging conditions that Blacks returned to after the war.

Because of this global nationalization within communities of colonial subjects, it is essential to establish the significant events of World War I and its impact on the Black diaspora. Therefore, chapter 1 looks outside of the American West to examine the global conditions that Blacks lived in before, during, and just after World War I. This analysis includes an examination of the ways in which the war educated Black populations, both in terms of reading and writing courses in US training camps and an increased opportunity for Black participants to learn more about the cross-cultural experience internationally. These experiences ultimately contributed to the rapid postwar rise of Garveyism and shaped the structure of racial nationalism in the subsequent generation.

Chapter 2 analyzes and interprets the Black experience on the West Coast along with other nationalist groups who also emerged in the West. Garveyism arose simultaneously as Southeast Asian, Japanese, and Mexican nationalisms also formed in the West. This chapter brings together these nationalist movements and provides evidence of their interactions and an analysis of their parallel circumstances.

At the heart of every nationalist movement is the desire for group economic independence. No industry represented this goal more than the maritime industry. Just as Indian[15] nationalism mobilized around the shipping industry, and as Chinese American nationalists attempted to own and operate their own shipping line, Garveyites also sought to form an international shipping line. Chapter 3 details the rise and fall of the Black Star Line in the context of other global nationalist attempts at establishing maritime commercial enterprises. For most Garvey historians, the failure of the Black Star Line represents the epitome of all that was wrong with Garvey and his movement. And though it cannot be denied that at times he made poor business decisions, it is unreasonable to lay all the blame for this failure at Garvey's feet. Given the hostility of the existing imperial administrations in Europe, past and current racist practices prevalent in the US, and the fierce competition from other already established shipping enterprises, the prospects for success for the Black Star Line were dubious at best.

Finally, chapter 4 details the decline of Garveyism in the American West. Although the decline of Garveyism in the West Coast urban areas is somewhat easy to examine thanks to the work of Emory Tolbert and others—as well as government surveillance of Garveyites and other nationalists in the cities—an examination of Garveyism in the rural towns is much more difficult to conduct because very little information on these towns has survived. This chapter seeks not only to determine the reasons that Garveyism in the cities declined but also to create a narrative of how Black nationalism may have existed in these rural towns and in what ways they may have interacted with other nationalist groups in the labor industries of the more rural and agricultural parts of the West.

There are many reasons to study the West Coast Garvey movement. Primarily, because the Black population was so small, the need for Garveyites to align with other nationalist groups became a necessity in the fight against white racial oppression. Indian nationalists, Japanese nationalists, and Mexican nationalists contended with the same racial issues in the American West that confronted the western Black population. Yet, these groups are rarely studied with an eye to their interracial organizing. By keeping all of these groups conceptually separate, scholars have lost an important historical moment of insight. Through their separation, the effects that European imperialism had on all nations of color in the World War I era is forgotten. India becomes a faraway British colony that had nothing to do with the United States and therefore not worth including in our national narrative while Japanese immigration to the United States is told as if Japanese immigrants fought anti-Asian laws in near total isolation from other groups of color in the prelude to World War II. Mexican American nationalism is discussed as if the discrimination and racial terrorism they suffered were unique to them in the American West—if it is discussed at all. Therefore, the Black experience in the West is often relegated to a footnote to all the larger immigrant populations of color. A coordinated examination of these groups that traces the ways in which they interacted, however, can begin to reveal the global interconnectedness of these historical events. The scholars' narrow viewpoint expands, and we see that Black nationalists credit the Japanese for their attempts to push for global racial equality after World War I; racist Asian exclusionary organizations resulted in the creation of a radical Indian nationalist movement in San Francisco; and Mexican American nationalists proposed organizing with Blacks in a bid for a separate state in the American Southwest. All of these connections are lost when the nationalist movements are treated in isolation.

Finally, and most importantly, the recognition and study of the Garvey movement as more than simply a Black Nationalist movement allows other historically oppressed racial groups to connect their own histories to this crucial, yet rarely acknowledged, moment in world history. When students of history can recognize the interracial character of these early nationalist movements in the proper context of what was a global movement against white oppression, they gain a fuller understanding of world events in the era. The successes and failures of historical multiracial organizing are significant, as Blacks, Asians, and Latinx still organize to fight for their rights in a country that was built on the struggle to maintain white supremacy, continuing through the civil rights era of the 1950s and 1960s through now in our contemporary era. Understanding the historical trajectory of how these groups have worked together—and the reasons they sometimes worked independently—can be useful in finding successful ways to come together in the current racial climate.

Methodologically, this proved to be a difficult book to write. There are few works that engage with the Black experience on the West Coast (especially in rural areas) during the World War I era because larger Black populations did not establish themselves in significant numbers in these locations until World War II. There is even less material on Garveyism on the West Coast, and yet still less that examines the interactions of nationalist groups of color in this region and time period. As a result, data collection proved difficult, and many conclusions must be surmised rather than proven outright as fact. The *Garvey Papers* and the Archives found in the Columbia Rare Book and Manuscripts Library, the Schomburg Center for

Research in Black Culture in New York, and the National Archives in Washington, DC, were the most valuable of resources to help put this story together, but they are by no means exhaustive. If this topic sparks the interest of readers, I hope more books will be written on this subject and time period in the future.

BLACK STAR RISING

1

THE RETURN
OF THE BLACK
SOLDIER

Marcus Garvey was by no means the first Black nationalist, nor was he the first Black leader to advocate Black pride, a "Back to Africa" movement, or a Black-owned and -operated shipping line. All these ideas had existed at least a century before Garvey. It was Garvey's cultivation of Black pride in the wake of World War I that created an environment in which his movement could experience an unprecedented expansion of growth and influence. The meteoric rise of Garveyism and his Universal Negro Improvement Association and African Communities League (UNIA) cannot be understood outside of the context of World War I, for without the events that transpired in that era, it is highly likely that Garveyism would have had little to no significant historical impact. To understand why World War I gave rise to the largest Black mass movement in world history, it is necessary to explore the circumstances in which Blacks found themselves prior to that event. For example, during a brief period after the Civil War from 1865 to 1877, which historians customarily refer to as Reconstruction, Blacks in the US experienced new ways of participating in US civil and political life. By the advent of World War I, this participation had devolved into a near slave-like condition due to the emergence of a comprehensive system of political, economic, and social inequality known as Jim Crow.[1]

In the United States, the era of Reconstruction had given newly freed Blacks a glimpse of what civil, political, and social equality might look like. Reconstruction had birthed a number of changes to the Constitution: the Thirteenth Amendment of 1865, which ended legal slavery (except as punishment for a crime); the Fourteenth Amendment of 1868, which gave Blacks citizenship and guaranteed all citizens equal protection under the law; and the Fifteenth Amendment of 1870, which declared that the right to vote could not be restricted based on race. The intent of these amendments was to provide a path to equality for Black people. In addition, the Civil Rights Acts of 1866 and 1875 defined citizenship and gave Blacks equal access to public accommodations and transportation. In order to support those newly granted rights, the Freedmen's Bureau, which was the first federal agency established to promote and ensure social welfare, created schools and hospitals; oversaw a contract labor system; and provided legal services to emancipated Blacks. Eventually, a virulent current of unrelenting opposition from the former slaveholding element effectively worked to subvert these hard-won advances.

The Freedmen's Bureau had success during its years of operation, but Congress dismantled it in 1872 in response to pressure from white southerners. In 1883, the Supreme Court overturned the Civil Rights Act of 1875. They argued that it was unconstitutional because Congress did not have the authority to require equal treatment by private companies. Finally, the case of *Plessy v. Ferguson*, in which a light-skinned Black man (Homer Plessy) challenged the racial segregation laws of Louisiana by taking a seat in the white section of a passenger train, established the legal concept of "separate but equal" as the law of the land in 1896. In practice, the "separate" portion of the concept was vigorously enforced while the "equal" portion was effectively ignored, a pattern that prevailed until long after the landmark *Brown v. Board of Education* ruling of the Supreme Court in 1954. The racial dynamics of the Reconstruction Era and integration of the former Black slave population into the country's social and economic fabric was further compromised between the end of the Civil War and the beginning of World War I by the large waves of white immigrants arriving from Europe.

Outside the court system, the methods used to enforce white supremacy were fierce, including political, social, and economic repression. These were ultimately enforced by the dominant white population's application of overt racial violence. Between 1885 and 1919, there were more than three thousand Black lynchings, mostly—but not exclusively—in the South.[2] Race riots and individual acts of violence helped reestablish white domination over Blacks. In 1908, a white riot in Springfield, Illinois, completely destroyed Black neighborhoods and businesses and prompted the establishment of the National Association for the Advancement of Colored People (NAACP). In 1917, the *St. Louis Argus* reported on a July 6 white riot in east St. Louis, calling it a "National Disgrace": white East St. Louis rioters "shot, tortured, and burned to death" nearly 100 Black people and destroyed more than 200 homes.[3]

Before World War I, racial inequality prevailed throughout the Western Hemisphere wherever large African descendent populations existed. These populations had been introduced into the Western Hemisphere during an era when European colonization and legalized slavery were in existence throughout the Caribbean and Central and South America. Although there was not a widespread tradition of mob violence in the Caribbean as there was in the American South, mechanisms of the state in such areas established rigid racial hierarchies, which typically involved the continuation of former colonial power structures dominated by the practices of white supremacy. The expansion of American imperialism into other parts of the hemisphere brought with it the spread of racial practices that mirrored those in the US while also reflecting the particularities of local racial histories.[4] By 1917, the year Woodrow Wilson brought the United States into World War I, the US had occupied Haiti and the Dominican Republic and controlled Cuba, as well as purchased the Danish Virgin Islands for twenty-five million dollars,[5] ostensibly to bring "democracy" to those areas but in reality to serve the interests of American corporate entities such as the United Fruit Company (UFC).

British colonial rule administered other islands in the Caribbean, such as Barbados, Jamaica, St. Kitts, and Trinidad and Tobago while France controlled Martinique and Guadeloupe. Under European colonial rule, the Caribbean islands continued the monoculture export economies based on Black labor that had been established in the colonies during slavery. Sugar, bananas, oil, timber, sponges, whale oil, and other products were extracted from the region and shipped around the world.[6] Whether through American military and political intrusion or the continuing European colonial control maintained well into the twentieth century, the realities of life, work, and civil rights for the region's Black populations reflected their political and economic exploitation under white supremacy in those areas.

The most notorious American corporation was the UFC. Active both in the Caribbean islands and on the Central American mainland, the company focused on banana cultivation. To construct the necessary infrastructure to support their agricultural activities, such as the construction of railroad lines, warehouses, etc., the UFC employed primarily Black West Indian labor. The original purpose for the banana plants was to feed labor crews constructing the national railroads, but it was quickly discovered that the fruit could be cultivated for a high profit. The company created plantations throughout the region, stimulating the need for cheap labor. As a result, large numbers of people migrated to Central America for work. Between 1900 and 1913, some 20,000 Jamaicans migrated to Costa Rica to work on the banana plantations there.[7] One such Jamaican, Marcus Garvey, worked for the company before World War I and understood firsthand the depth of exploitation of which the UFC was capable.

In 1910, as many other Jamaicans had done, Garvey relocated from Jamaica to Limón, Costa Rica, where he found employment working for the UFC as a timekeeper; it was the lowest position in Central America a white man could have,[8] but the highest that a Black man could attain. And although there were thousands of Caribbean migrants induced to labor on the Panama Canal in this era, by 1910 at least 20,000 British West Indians were diverted to Limón.[9] Many of these migrants were employed by the UFC, which made it a point to use West Indians as its primary labor source. Because the UFC was an American-owned company based in Boston, it imported to that region American-style patterns of Jim Crow race relations. Segregation and a general lack of respect for Black life were the rule. Enforcement of Jim Crow could be both brutal and violent. When necessary, for example, indigenous locals could be hired to rid the company of any West Indians who refused to comply with the system. As one UFC white plantation manager explained, "On my plantation was a native who would for the sum of ten dollars remove any negro from sight and no questions asked. The only stipulation he made was that the designated man be given work near the river. The deed was quietly done and the body slipped into the river where the alligators removed all evidence of the crime."[10]

Work conditions mirrored the harsh enforcement methods. Accidental West Indian deaths on the job were largely ignored. One white visitor to the region stated after learning that six Jamaican workers died in a fall from a faulty cable, "none of the bodies were ever found, and my informant didn't seem to care."[11] This lack of concern for worker health was equally prevalent when dealing with disease and other medical exigencies. Black West Indians did the most difficult and dangerous work involved in cultivation and production on the banana plantations and were paid far less than whites while working long hours in the hot, damp tropical climate of the jungle. The average daily temperature on a banana plantation was eighty degrees with high humidity and continuous rains which could accumulate as much as twenty inches or more in summer months. In places like Costa Rica, banana plantation workers combated the world's deadliest spider, the banana spider, which hides in the leaves of banana plants,[12] as well as fourteen different species of scorpion, twenty-two different species of venomous snake, vampire bats, fire ants—an aggressive species that attacks en masse and whose venomous bite causes a sensation of being on fire—and, most deadly of all, disease-spreading mosquitoes. In other plantation regions such as Honduras, workers faced all of this in addition to bullet ants, whose bite is so painful it is said the recipient feels as if they have been shot with a gun. Labor unrest was a predictable consequence of the harsh conditions. In 1910, Black workers went on strike in Costa Rica, motivating the UFC to employ Hispanic workers in order to break the strike.[13] This move proved unsuccessful, but it worked to foster a community of racial solidarity among Black workers.

Angered by the treatment of West Indians in the region, in 1911, Garvey established *La Nación,* a small newspaper that challenged the practices of UFC employers and their associates. Local white firefighters, whom he had accused of allowing West Indian businesses to burn down, destroyed his printing press in that same year. The UFC, irritated by his attempts at labor organizing, refused to come to his aid.[14] After the destruction of his newspaper, Garvey was ready to move on. However, it wasn't just his burned newspaper that caused him to leave. Garvey's finances were in crisis. He had used advertisements in his newspaper to raise funds for a celebration of King George's coronation. He had also accumulated debts when he established his printing press. He left without completing payment of those debts and residents accused him of absconding with funds raised for a celebration that never took place.[15] If true, these accusations against Garvey represent early forewarnings of the kind of mismanagement that would later plague his UNIA movement and initiate the decline of his influence in the US.

From Costa Rica he moved on to British Honduras, where he roused audiences with his charismatic speaking style. He resided for a brief period during 1911 in Colón, Panama. In 1913, he traveled around Europe and worked briefly with the well-known actor, African nationalist, and journalist, Dusé Mohamed Ali, contributing to the latter's political newspaper, the *African Times and Orient Review*. While on his travels, Garvey read Booker T. Washington's *Up from Slavery*, which inspired him to create an organization that could motivate Blacks around the world to come together for the purpose of self-rule and economic freedom from white domination.[16]

Two months after Garvey left England in June of 1914 to return to Jamaica, Great Britain declared war on Germany. Like many colonial subjects, Garvey supported England at the onset of the war. Feeling it would be better to remain colonized by the English than to be recolonized by the Germans, Garvey stated in a press release from his first UNIA in Jamaica that Black members "sincerely pray for the success of British Arms on the battlefields of Europe and Africa, and 'at Sea, in crushing the 'common Foe,' the enemy of peace and further civilization.'"[17] Such conflicting loyalties confronted the Black population in the US as well as in the rest of the hemisphere on the eve of World War I. The circumstances created by that global conflict, cast in the rhetoric of the US and its allies as the war for "democracy," would create the environment in which Garvey would build his Black nationalist movement after the war. The war also energized an anti-colonial movement throughout the European empires, including in Africa, Southeast Asia, China, and, to an extent, Japan. On the West Coast of the United States, this anti-colonial movement eventually aligned Black nationalists with other groups from colonized regions and put into play the dynamics that would make the Garvey movement in the American West very different from the movement as practiced in the eastern, northern, and southern areas of the US as well as throughout the Caribbean Basin.

Between July 1914 and November 1918, over eight million soldiers died during the European countries' battle over world domination. In the United States, many Blacks had no desire to participate in a war for democracy while living in a country in which they had few democratic rights. However, there were many others who were convinced that by participating in military service they might successfully prove themselves worthy of the equal rights they had lost after Reconstruction and believed that the exercise of their patriotism would erase racial oppression. There existed a hope that whites might see their efforts, admit that their own racial bias was incorrect, and then reward Blacks and other people of color with racial equality. However, this approach did not have universal support in Black America: not all Black soldiers entered the war by choice. Some Blacks evaded military service by fleeing to Canada or Mexico to avoid compulsory participation through the draft, which President Woodrow Wilson had put in place one month after the United States entered the war.

Draft boards, most of which were made up exclusively of whites, had no problem pressing Blacks into service over whites seeking to avoid service. For example, "the local draft board in Fulton County, Georgia, exempted 526 of 815 white registrants but only 6 of over 200 African Americans. [In fact] thirteen percent of all draftees were black, even though blacks constituted slightly less than ten percent of the American population."[18]

Blacks did not constitute the only group of color in the United States to suffer disproportionate draft call-ups. American Indigenous, Mexican Americans, and Mexican nationals were also drafted into World War I. The requirement for each county to provide a certain quota of eligible Black and white participants based on population makeup meant that filling the white quota in those areas where

Black populations were prevalent would require a change in how race was constructed, at least on paper. Therefore, the racial classification of American Indigenous and Mexicans as white became a significant factor. For example, some counties in North Carolina had a majority of Black residents and not enough white registrants were available to fill the quota. To solve the problem, the governor classified fifty-seven of its Lumbee Indigenous residents as white.[19] Approximately 25 percent of the adult male Indigenous population served alongside whites during the war[20] even though indigenous peoples were not considered citizens and found themselves fighting for a country that did not recognize them. Similarly, Mexican Americans and Mexican nationals also held a confusing status in the US. Although noncitizens were technically not legally allowed to be drafted, as in the case with American Indigenous, draft boards took their own liberties in determining who was a citizen and who was not according to their quota needs. It "is estimated that as many as 200,000 non-declarant aliens were illegally drafted and nine percent of the American Expeditionary Force were non-citizens."[21] In the early months of the registration process, draft cards did not include boxes for marking a person's racial status. Therefore, in order to keep those who were determined as "white" separate from Blacks, the corners were torn on cards to indicate that a registrant was Black.[22] Unlike Black Americans, who were relegated primarily to labor, American Indigenous, Mexican Americans, and Mexican nationals (regardless of citizenship) were put on the front lines of the war and expected to fight and die alongside whites.

Of the 4.3 million Americans mobilized in World War I (drafted or otherwise), approximately 400,000 were Black. When Blacks could not run away to avoid the draft, some simply deserted. In the South, where Black draftees were treated so callously, "African Americans constituted twenty-two percent, or 105,831 of the 474,861 reported draft deserters." It comes as no surprise that more than 60 percent of these deserters came from the American South.[23]

11

In 1914, there were four all-Black regiments in the Army: the 9th and 10th colored cavalry and the 24th and 25th colored infantry regiments. Combined, they totaled about 10,000 soldiers, and although only a third of them would be shipped overseas in World War I, all four units had participated in the Spanish-American War in 1898. Recognizing that no wartime participation had resulted in Black equality, Black radical Chandler Owen, a law student at Columbia and future co-editor of the popular Black socialist newspaper *The Messenger*, wrote, "Did not the Negro take part in the Spanish–American War only to be discharged without honors and without a hearing by the president who rose into political prestige and power upon their valor in that war? And have not prejudice and race hate grown in this country since 1898?"[24] Other Black leaders of the era, such as W.E.B. Du Bois, urged Blacks to support WWI and "to put [their] special grievances aside" in support of their country.[25] In Black communities, leadership splintered over whether or not Black Americans should support the war, especially as they had to contend with harsh treatment from their own government while fighting overseas for a country that refused to protect them at home. Conflicting opinions about Black participation eventually would be one of the factors that created an opportunity for Garvey to build his nationalist movement in the American Black community.

When the US entered the war in April 1917, Black American soldiers often received harsh treatment as well as substandard equipment—or no equipment at all. Conscripted and volunteered Black soldiers of the 365th, 366th, 367th, and 368th Regiments represented the 92nd Division.[26] The other all-Black division was the 93rd Division, made up of the 369th, 370th, 371st, and 372nd Regiments. Black American egiments were consigned to the dirtiest and most difficult work. For example, upon their arrival in France, the 368th Regiment in "a single day . . . unloaded 42,000 men with their portable gear." Black American "laborers quarried stone for roads, built and repaired railroads, cut and stacked firewood, and unloaded everything from 100-pound sacks of flour to 90-ton naval guns. At the port of Brest, they unloaded almost 800,000 tons of war material during the month of September 1918 alone."[27] Indeed, the near exclusive utilization of Black soldiers as wartime manual labor by the American Expeditionary Force and the unwillingness of white commanders to employ Blacks in combat capacities—perhaps due to a reluctance to have Blacks engage in killing whites in the name of democracy—led some Black soldiers to begin to question the wisdom of their decision to support the war effort. Eventually, most of those Blacks who engaged in official combat did so while assigned to the French Army after it became clear that if Blacks were used in the American forces, the conflict between them and their white American counterparts might exceed that with the official enemy. White soldiers, especially those from the South, sought to impose the American traditions of Jim Crow racism upon Black troops.

Yet, these Black troops, regardless of the workload they were given, were an impressive lot. New York City had one of the most famous Black regiments. In 1917, the year that Garvey's UNIA was formally established in Harlem with the opening of Liberty Hall (the official meeting place of the UNIA in Harlem), Colonel William Hayward endeavored to train Black men who had previously worked as elevator operators, waiters, or other low-level service positions. In the absence of actual weapons, the men trained with wooden sticks.[28] The regiment later became known as the Harlem Hellfighters and saw battle in both World War I and World War II. Their performance in combat belied the negative stereotypes whites commonly ascribed to them.

While some Black soldiers fought on the battlefields of Europe, the majority of Black recruits in the United States were not shipped overseas. Most stayed on American soil, where working conditions for Black American soldiers closely mirrored prison chain gangs. Advertisements seeking white officers to run these gangs were published in local newspapers. These advertisements often closely resembled the ones put out only half a century earlier when a slave owner needed an overseer. One such advertisement out of Florida read: "Non-Commissioned Officers Wanted. White Men. Married or single. Experienced in the Handling of Colored Men."[29] It was believed that Black men in general were incapable of managing themselves and that it was necessary for whites to manage Blacks in order to get any work out of them. Once they volunteered (or were compelled) to join the military, Black troops who remained on US soil were not issued military uniforms because to see a Black man in an Army uniform inflamed white racists and therefore affected the safety of the soldier. Instead, they had to wear overalls and could be verbally abused or even assaulted by white officers. According to one soldier who labored at Fort Jackson in South Carolina: "the Captain beat us with sticks and whip and give the non-commission officers the authority to beat or kill any of us negro that don't do what they say and they will give him a five or ten day furlow [sic] for doing so . . . our captain told us we are not soldiers, that all niggers are made to work."[30]

When the war was over, Black soldiers stationed in the Southern states were denied release from the Army and were forced to continue the work of digging ditches, building roads and railroads, and other kinds of hard labor. When these Black soldiers asked to be relieved from duty, the government denied their requests, claiming that their continued service was too important to the country. Overseas, Black troops were forced to stay in France longer than whites to bury dead soldiers, yet "despite miserable living conditions and the horrors of the task they managed to locate and bury over 23,000 bodies" in various stages of decomposition.[31] Although the French treated Black troops with relative respect, most of their white American counterparts endeavored to maintain the inequitable racial status quo overseas.

Back in New York, W.E.B. Du Bois, upon hearing of the bravery of Black troops, wrote an article titled "Close Ranks" in 1918. The article, published in *The Crisis*, the official publication of the NAACP, urged Blacks to "let us, while this war lasts, forget our special grievances and close our ranks shoulder to shoulder with our own white fellow citizens and the allied nations that are fighting for democracy."[32] Black radical leaders such as Hubert Harrison and A. Philip Randolph pounced on this article, which they interpreted as Du Bois' acquiescence to lynching, disenfranchisement, and Jim Crow segregation. It is important to note that during the war, Garvey was not yet considered one of the popular Black leaders in the United States (as were Du Bois and Booker T. Washington in the late nineteenth and early twentieth centuries). Around the time the US entered the war, Garvey was living in abject poverty in Harlem and had started his first UNIA chapter with only thirteen members. He was respected by many of his contemporaries—although, due to intraracial competition for leadership within the Black community, that circumstance was not to last—but though he was gaining some popularity among Black audiences in Harlem, he would not emerge as the leader of the largest Black mass movement in world history until 1919, with the return of the Black soldier.

Rather, in 1917, Garvey was aligned with Hubert Harrison, although he commanded a much smaller influence in the ranks of Black leadership than Harrison at that time. Harrison, also known as the "Black Socrates" because of his ability to lecture brilliantly on a broad range of topics, wrote the first ever comprehensive analysis of Blacks and socialism in the United States;[33] he pioneered the soapbox speaker tradition utilized by radicals like A. Philip Randolph and Malcolm X; and he was one of the first to insist upon the capitalization of the word Negro in newspapers and other publications. To him racism was neither innate nor the natural order of things; it was a learned behavior that could be unlearned. Coincidentally, decades before Du Bois published his famous work

Black Reconstruction in1935, Harrison had worked diligently on his own book of the same title in 1907, sensing the need for an account of Reconstruction in the South from the Black viewpoint.[34] And in the Black radical tradition, long before the emergence of the Black Panthers and Nelson Mandela, Harrison promoted armed self-defense and sabotage against racial enemies.

Upon reading Du Bois' article, "Close Ranks," Harrison responded swiftly. That same month, in July 1918, Harrison wrote:

> Let us assume that we consent to being lynched - "during the war" - and submit tamely and with commendable weakness to being Jim-crowed and disenfranchised. Very well. Will not that be of our spirit and of its quality? Of course. And what you *call* that spirit won't alter its quality, will it? Now, ask all the peoples of all the world what they call a people who smilingly consent to their own degradation and destruction. They are called cowards - because they *are* cowards. In America we call such people "niggers."[35]

In a slightly more moderate tone, in their radical socialist newspaper, *The Messenger*, Chandler Owen and A. Philip Randolph responded to Du Bois, stating, "No intelligent Negro is willing to lay down his life for the United States as it now exists. Intelligent Negroes have now reached the point where their support for the country is conditional."[36]

Garvey used this debate over the role of Blacks in the war effort to elevate his visibility. Like Du Bois, who later would become his most strident enemy in the struggle for Black leadership, Garvey advocated Black service in the war effort. Yet, he did so for a very different reason than Du Bois: Du Bois had advocated Black service as a pathway to white acceptance. Garvey, in contrast, proclaimed that Black service would lead to young Black men's acquisition of the military skills that could be turned to the fight against white oppression on the home front after the war. According to a New York City police report, Garvey "addressed a meeting on the west side of Lenox Avenue between 135th and 136th Streets, from 9:10

to 10:30 pm," where he proclaimed to a large audience that the Black man should go to war and learn how to use the bayonet and the gun. He should learn how to use them "so that if the white man slaps his face he can use his gun and bayonet on him and put the white man under the ground."[37] Such rhetoric makes it clear why Garvey stood out from the rest of the Black leaders after the war. Garvey's message had heat to it—a message of violent self-defense and revenge—and it ignited a fire in those who heard it. Such a message came to resonate with a Black population eager for some of that democracy they had fought for overseas to materialize in their lives at home.

Throughout the war years, Garvey worked to inspire Black resistance to whites in a variety of ways. In the summer of 1917, a race riot broke out in East St. Louis in response to the nearly 500 Black workers hired to replace white strikers at the Aluminum Ore Company. By the time the National Guard was called in to do what the local police refused to do—protect Black citizens—more than one hundred Blacks had been murdered. In response to this horrific event, W.E.B. Du Bois led a silent march of protest in New York City. Garvey, on the other hand, took a different approach and accused the US government of conspiring against Blacks in St. Louis, most of whom had migrated from the South in search of better wages. From his podium in Harlem, he exclaimed: "At one time it was slavery, at another time lynching and burning, and up to date it is whole[sale] butchering. This is a crime against the laws of humanity; it is a crime against the laws of the nation; it is a crime against Nature; and a crime against the God of all mankind!"[38]

This type of reaction resonated with his audiences and with his readers. Throughout the war years and after, he made statements along similar lines, urging Blacks to take up arms and fight for their rights. Representative examples of his rhetoric included: "For every Negro lynched by Whites in the South the Negroes ought to lynch a White man in the North";[39] "If Negroes can face death to procure the liberties of white peoples, then Negroes can face death to procure the liberties of black peoples";[40] and "The time for the peaceful penetration of the black man's right by the white man is past, and the time for a determined resistance has come."[41] In these speeches, which were published on the front pages of the *Negro World* (the official organ of the UNIA), Garvey proclaimed what many Blacks were already feeling in the war's aftermath.

This impulse captured by Garvey to rise up and fight against white oppression ultimately propelled Garveyism into what would become bigger than the individual himself. It was not an unprecedented impulse. It had seen earlier incarnations in the slave revolts of Haiti as well as in the slave insurrections of Denmark Vesey, Gabriel Prosser, Nat Turner, and many others. On the individual level, it had materialized in the actions of slaves who killed or fought back against their masters, as Frederick Douglass did in beating down the slave breaker hired to break his spirit of independence. However, the circumstances created by the war years and evolving racial realities of the early twentieth century were the right catalyst for Garvey to grow that impulse into the first large-scale Black nationalist movement to shake the country—and the world—at the end of World War I.

Beyond the streets of Harlem and outside of the US, Blacks in the rest of the Western Hemisphere in large part shared similar World War I experiences. These shared experiences ultimately led to similar postwar reactions that drove Black people all over the world over to join the Garvey movement. Just as in the United States, Blacks in the Caribbean had a variety of reactions to the war. Probably even more than in the US, large numbers of West Indians in the Caribbean under the British Crown wanted to participate in the war to show their allegiance to the mother country, even as they were oppressed by their colonizers.

In the West Indies, the British military initially refused to take Black soldiers into its ranks. According to one historian, "despite the impressive record of the West Indies Regiments, who had served in numerous colonial and imperial campaigns since the American War of Independence, black soldiers were regarded as lacking the necessary self-control and intelligence to cope with the demands of modern warfare."[42] When the all-Black British West Indian Regiment (BWIR) was finally permitted to serve in the Great War, they were regarded as "natives" and not citizens. Therefore, they were paid less than their white counterparts. Furthermore, they were banned from modes of entertainment and places of social interaction such as movie houses and restaurants. They were segregated in regiments and hospitals, and in some cases were treated worse than prisoners of war. This treatment of the Black West Indian soldier during wartime came to represent a shared experience of nearly all Blacks who participated in the war. Such international shared exposure to the plight of Black peoples in general heightened the awareness for the need of a global Black nationalist movement.

Events on the white side of the color line also contributed to the racial climate during and after the war years that worked to heighten racial tension and invoke the postwar climate that paved the way for a turn to Garveyism by many Black Americans. The Ku Klux Klan, a white racist terrorist group that rode throughout the South terrorizing and lynching newly freed slaves following the Civil War, went underground after Congress authorized federal suppression of the group in 1871. Regardless of the group's suppression, the end of Reconstruction in 1876 saw the role of the Klan in the South become largely absorbed into the official offices and functions of state and local government. This "officialization" of white supremacy and Black repression meant that typical Klan activities like night riding, cross burnings, etc., were no longer as widespread, with the exception of incidents of occasional mob violence. This also made the traditional Klan less visible as legal Jim Crow took hold in the country. The changing racial and social conditions emerging in the early decades of the twentieth century, however, worked to destabilize in the eyes of many whites, especially in the South, the preferred racial status quo. The urbanization of society in the North and the ceasing of European immigration by the outbreak of World War I provided new opportunities for dissatisfied southern Blacks, generating a Black urban migration to the North that would transform both northern and southern sections of the country in profound ways.[43] The emergence of a growing Black middle and professional class and the increasing success of the protest organizations they created also threatened dramatic challenges to the old racial status quo.

Within this environment of change, the country was ripe for whites to appeal for a return to the old ways of establishing the white Protestant dominance that had worked in earlier generations. With the release of D. W. Griffith's silent film *Birth of a Nation* in 1915, the Klan experienced a rapid revitalization in the South that spread quickly throughout the country. The film, which was based on a book called *The Clansman* by Thomas Dixon, had been refashioned into a play before it was made into the one of the most famous films of all time. Its three-hour epic narrative included the story of how the Ku Klux Klan rose up after the Civil War to save the white South from Black buffoons who ate fried chicken on the floor of the State Legislature and whose primary objective was to have sex with white women. The real-life version of the Klan's agenda was expanded to include the need to control the dangers of any "un-American" religious or social group like immigrant Catholic populations and other religious or other groups of a threatening ethnic persuasion, such as Jews, Mexicans, Chinese, Japanese, and any other groups perceived to be a concern to white Protestant Americanism.

This latest version of the KKK became extremely popular and soon permeated government offices in many parts of the United States. Among the Klan's members were doctors, lawyers, police officers, congressmen, senators, poor whites, middle-class whites, and wealthy whites. President Woodrow Wilson, a Southern Democrat and close personal friend of Thomas Dixon and D. W. Griffith, played *The Birth of a Nation* in the White House for high-level politicians and diplomats. According to Chalmers, "the Southern-born President was much moved. [He is reported to have said] 'It is like writing history with lightning, and my only regret is that it is all so terribly true.'"[44] Not long afterwards, the Chief Justice of the Supreme Court, Justice Edward White, in an interview with Thomas Dixon, admitted to having been a member of the Klan and looked forward to the film's release which promised to tell the "true story" of the rise of the Klan.[45] In 1922, the rebirth of the Klan would play an ironic role as a factor in Garvey's decline after he met semi-clandestinely with the Grand Dragon of the Klan in Georgia.

The hyper-racialized environment of wartime America, further excited by films like *Birth of a Nation* and the visible prominence of the "new" Klan with the inflammatory racial messages they encouraged, greatly affected the negative wartime experiences of many young Black men in the military. White officers at the highest levels of the military spread rumors accusing Black soldiers of the 92nd Division of raping white French women. As a result, members of the 92nd and 93rd regiments became targets for racist soldiers and officers as well as for the white American public.[46] The severity of the issues, along with the letters that Black soldiers consistently wrote to the NAACP begging for help, inspired W.E.B. Du Bois to travel to France in 1919 and investigate the plight of the 92nd Division. His investigation culminated in a damning exposé which he published in *The Crisis*, revealing just how poorly Black American troops were treated in France by a racist American government. In his exposé Du Bois wrote, "On one subject the white Commanding Officers of all colored units showed more solicitude than on the organization and fighting efficiency of the troops,—that was the relations of the colored officers and men with the women of France. They began by officially stigmatizing the Negroes as rapists; then solemnly warned the troops in speeches and general order not even to speak to women on the street; ordered the white military police to spy on the blacks and arrest them if they found them talking with French women."[47] Furthermore, Du Bois highlighted that the majority of commanding officers over Black troops were white men from the South who were thought to be able to "handle Negroes" more effectively. He found that in spite of the fact that "French law and custom stepped in repeatedly to protect them," there was nothing to be done because under Southern commanders Blacks were "worked often like slaves, twelve to fourteen hours a day, these men were ill-fed, poorly clad, indifferently housed, often beaten, always 'Jim-Crowed' and insulted."[48] At the end of the war, Black soldiers who had participated in battle, fought bravely, and even gained the respect in many cases of their white officers were barred from participation in parades and award ceremonies in France.

Recognizing how Black soldiers were treated during the war regardless of the country or region they had come from is crucial to understanding national and international Black reactions after the war. One of the principal factors to consider when analyzing the Black experience in World War I is that Europeans used their Black colonial subjects to fight the war at the same time, continuing to treat them as noncitizens. African and Caribbean colonial subjects were relegated to the same demeaning jobs on the warfront as Black Americans from the United States, and therefore the two groups often came into intimate contact with one another in France. Approximately 135,000 Black soldiers came from Africa alone. Many came from places such as Algeria, Morocco, and Tunisia in Northern Africa.[49] When Blacks from around the world met in the labor camps in Europe, African Americans sometimes held the same prejudices and stereotypes of Africans as their white counterparts, and communication across language barriers initially created an impediment. As Black Americans and Africans had more contact with each other, many of these barriers were overcome. Blacks on an international level understood their shared experiences both as laborers in the war and as an oppressed people at home.[50] This would become a key component in the global popularity of the Garvey movement. Upon their return, it became clear very quickly to many African Americans that Blacks the world over were no longer willing to accept the old patterns of race relations that had existed prior to the war.[51]

Throughout the Caribbean, the United States, and the world, the return of Black soldiers from World War I intensified Black resistance to white oppression. Black veterans, who had performed heroically in battle and loyally in service, were fed up with the old racial system. After the war many Blacks found themselves unemployed, unappreciated, and economically desperate. Blacks had changed during the war, but the oppressive conditions with which they contended had remained much the same. As a result, in 1919, race riots broke out on both sides of the Atlantic, as well as in the Caribbean Basin. In the postwar years, in just a matter of a few short months, Garvey's UNIA established more than a thousand chapters throughout the world, as many returning Black veterans turned to Garveyism to organize and resist white oppression. The experiences Blacks had in World War I and the subsequent issues they were forced to deal with upon their return accounted for the variations that the Garvey movement experienced in the Western Hemisphere. As will be explored throughout this book, by the end of 1919, Garveyism had less to do with Marcus Garvey the individual and more to do with a multifaceted campaign in pursuit of racial progress within the diversity of locations in which Black populations operated. In the American West, that pursuit eventually came to include non-Black peoples as well.

In the West Indies, the issues that created the rise of Garveyism focused almost exclusively on labor conditions and the new attitude of returning soldiers, which ultimately led to strikes and race riots. West Indian veterans, such as those of the Black West Indian Regiment, came back from the war disheartened by their treatment within the British Empire. News quickly traveled back to the

Caribbean of the racial violence against former Black soldiers who were barred from employment in Great Britain, leading to race riots in Wales, Newport, London, Barry, Liverpool, and Cardiff. These riots, and the horrifying tales of violence against Black veterans, had far-reaching consequences throughout the Empire.

The *Negro World* carried Garvey's speeches and his "by any means necessary" call to arms to more than forty countries around the world. The newspaper traveled by rail, steamboat, ship, car, foot, and horseback. In July 1919, for example, "reports of gangs of white soldiers and sailors 'savagely attacking, beating, and stabbing every negro they could find' in the streets of Liverpool, including a Trinidadian, Charles Wooten" sparked racial protest and violence in Belize, British Honduras, and Trinidad.[52] Simultaneously, fearing that Garvey's *Negro World* was contributing to this racial violence, the colonial governments declared the newspaper either banned outright or suppressed in Belize, British Honduras, Jamaica, St. Vincent, Costa Rica, and all of the West Indian islands. In the following year, the Bahamas and all of the Windward Islands followed suit.[53] The suppression of the *Negro World* in the Western Hemisphere and in colonial Africa in fact stimulated more violence and helped to popularize the Garvey movement, especially in the Caribbean Basin.[54]

Further north in the United States (the *Negro World* was not banned in the US), the summer of 1919 came to be known as the Red Summer due to the waves of bloody race riots that spread throughout the country in more than twenty cities, which included Chicago, New York, Washington, and Omaha, as well as Charleston, South Carolina; Norfolk, Virginia; Knoxville, Tennessee; Longview, Texas; and Elaine, Arkansas.[55] Most riots were in fact white mobs invading Black neighborhoods. Previously such terrorist attacks upon Black neighborhoods saw few repercussions for members of the racist mobs. But after the war, Black soldiers were not going to acquiesce to the same racial structures they had been forced to live in before the war. In Washington, DC, where one riot took place, a Black woman wrote: "The Washington riots gave me the thrill that comes once in a lifetime. I was alone when I read between the lines of the morning paper that at last our men had stood like men, struck back, were no longer dumb, driven cattle. . . . The pent-up humiliation, grief, and horror of a lifetime—half a century—was being stripped from me."[56]

These words reflect the New Negro of the twentieth century. As a result of World War I, the New Negro movement emphasized militant mass action self-defense, internationalism, racial pride, and economic self-sufficiency. All of these were necessary for the achievement of social justice and empowerment for Blacks. The New Negro was a departure from the older Black generation. Unlike the Old Negro, the New Negroes were radical and ready to take up arms. They refused to passively lie down and take what whites had to give them. In addition to the Blacks killed in the 1919 Washington, DC, riot, whites were killed as well by Black men, many of them former veterans who took to the streets with guns.[57] This new reality—Black self-defense—made race rioting a distinctly different affair from the race rioting of the prewar era. This changing racial landscape was in part the creation of Garvey and his movement and concurrently a big factor in Garvey and the UNIA's propulsion to a major element in the emerging local, national, and global racial developments of the postwar era.

In the Caribbean Basin, where Garvey's movement was the most popular, a variety of economic factors attracted Black participation in Garveyism. During World War I, companies such as the UFC, which had been the largest employer of West Indian labor, significantly reduced their production and distribution activities. Because of the war there was a substantial increase in imports and a decrease in exports from the islands. Fruit exports to the United States, specifically bananas, declined by one third. And, as a result of these changes, the cost of food in the islands inflated drastically, increasing upwards of 100 percent on some foods items.[58] For Black veterans returning from the war, these issues created considerable tension and poverty, exacerbated racial violence, and helped to push Blacks towards a nationalist agenda. Thus, Garveyism in the Caribbean Basin did not become as widespread as it had in the US until the end of World War I because frustrated Black soldiers and exploited Black laborers alike became desperate for a program that they could rally around. Members of the BWIR had become disillusioned by the time they came home and realized that change would not occur, even after they had risked their lives for the colonizer. As a result of this disenchantment, race consciousness spread rapidly throughout the Caribbean.[59] This disillusionment led to widespread labor unrest, and as former BWIR troops returned to a labor force that perpetuated the same racist values they experienced in Europe while providing unequal pay and long hours, they began to organize and strike.

Many of the West Indians who had fought in the war and returned to become strike leaders were the same men who organized UNIA chapters. Consequently, there was a direct connection between labor organizing, military service, and Garveyism in the Caribbean. In 1919, for example, West Indians employed by the Panama Canal and Panama Railroad Company went on strike. According to Ewing, "prominent in the agitation were several important Garveyites, all founding members of Panama's first UNIA division."[60] Furthermore:

> In the Windward Islands of St. Vincent, St. Lucia and Grenada, months of agitation by local Garveyites erupted in a strike of labourers and policemen in St. Lucia that threatened to spread into a general strike before the situation was calmed by a British warship. That same month, [another] massive strike—involving as many as 16,000 workers—was called in the Panama Canal Zone, this time led by Garveyites and supported directly by Marcus Garvey, who cabled $500 for the cause.[61]

Garveyism and the demand for Black rights had become a major characteristic in the labor battles of the Western Hemisphere.

In general, oppressive laws and practices by white colonizers and corporations made the Caribbean region a hotbed for labor organizing and strikes. Believing that Black West Indians were inherently lazy unless forced to work, the English colonial government in Trinidad and Tobago created the Habitual Idlers Ordinance in 1919. The ordinance "provided that any male habitually abstaining from work might be committed to a government-run agricultural settlement to be taught 'habits of industry'—and, when feasible, farmed out to private employers."[62] Though there is no evidence this ordinance was widely enforced, its language and provisions clearly reveal the nature of white intentions to preserve the presence of cheap Black labor. Throughout the Caribbean, these issues further motivated Black labor organizing and invigorated organizations like the UNIA, which were conceived to be effective mechanisms to subvert manifestations of white supremacy.

Beyond the UNIA itself, there were other organizations to which Garveyism became an important factor. One such organization was the Trinidad Workingmen's Association (TWA). The TWA was a West Indian labor organization begun by middle-class Blacks in 1897. By 1919, its membership included veterans of the First World War who were also Garveyites inspired by Garvey's message. This group promoted strikes of the longshoremen and stevedores who wanted higher wages and an eight-hour workday.[63] Due to the violence that ensued during the strikes as well as their ability to successfully put a halt to all normal shipping activity in Port-of-Spain, the colonial office was forced to compromise. Ironically, Garvey actually spoke out against such labor organizing when he visited the Caribbean on a speaking tour in 1921. Yet, this did not seem to deter West Indian labor organizers from supporting the Garvey movement, showing again that Garveyism had become much larger than Garvey the individual by this time.

While the TWA strike ensued in Trinidad, Samuel Haynes, a World War I veteran who fought in Egypt and who when he returned became secretary of the UNIA in Belize, led a race revolt in Belmopan.[64] Circumstances on the ground in the post-war Caribbean clearly reflected the appeal that Garveyism held for a more aggressive, militant Black response to white attempts at exploitation. Local circumstances determined that labor strife would provide much of the battlefield for that Black activism. Garveyites involved in those struggles adapted the strategies of Garveyism most appropriate to their localities. This was a pattern of adaptation to local circumstances that would play out again and again as the Garvey movement spread in the postwar years from areas as far-flung as West African colonies to the urban centers of the American West.

In the American South, many Black veterans were unable to escape the chain gang–like conditions they had experienced in the Army. Now no longer within the Army, Black workers attempted to unionize in order to protest white labor exploitation practices. Because these southern organizations also often drew on returning soldiers from World War I, 80 percent of UNIA divisions and chapters were organized in a two-year period, between 1919 and 1921.[65] Blacks working on the ships transported the *Negro World* to stevedores and dock workers who worked in the port cities, bringing UNIA organizations to the southern shorelines in places like Mobile, Alabama; Charleston, South Carolina; and New Orleans. Frustration with racist employers motivated Black union members such as those in the International Longshoreman's Association to join the UNIA.[66]

From the shorelines, Garveyism spread to the southern interior. Tenant farmers and sharecroppers also wanted to organize. Such attempts did not often produce positive results for the tenant farmers on the cotton and tobacco plantations of the rural South. One example is in the events that transpired in Elaine, Arkansas, where Black sharecroppers attempted to organize a union and bring suit against the white landowners for unpaid labor. Through the Progressive Farmers and Household Union of America, sixty-eight

Black residents organized and hired a white law firm from Little Rock, Arkansas.[67] The white plantation owners of Elaine, as on many plantations in the South, owned the stores where tenant farmers purchased food and household items and sold these items at inflated prices. They also profited heavily by taking the cotton to market and pocketing the majority of the proceeds from the crop. Furthermore, many sharecroppers would be forced to wait months before the white farmer paid out any share of the proceeds. After World War I, some Black sharecroppers determined to withhold the cotton until their landlords paid them the money owed. They also armed themselves in preparation for white retaliation. When whites received word of this, they took violent action. In the worst race riot in Arkansas history, five whites and dozens of Blacks were killed. In spite of this riot, a heavy white oppressive presence, and the losses suffered by the Black community—or more likely because of these circumstances—shortly thereafter, more than thirty UNIA chapters were organized within a fifty-mile radius of Elaine.[68]

Blacks in the American South did have very real things to fear. Lynching, mob violence, and the threat of death were realities within the scope of daily interracial interactions. Lynching was a frequent form of racial terrorism in the early twentieth century. As Black veterans returned from the war, some still choosing to wear their uniforms, angry whites reacted. A May 1919 article in the *Chicago Defender* reported several such incidents: "Daniel Mack, a returned soldier, who saw service overseas with the 365th Infantry, was taken from the city jail by four white men and beaten to death."[69] The offense that had put him in jail for thirty days was that while wearing his uniform he purportedly told a white man on the street that "he fought for the white man in France and would stand no mistreatment."[70] In Montgomery, Alabama, Robert Grosky, a Black soldier, and another man were "shot to death by a mob of 25 white men"[71] after they were released in the woods and ordered to "run." In the same town that month, "Ben Miller, a former soldier, was set upon by a gang of white men as he was walking on a main street downtown. He suffered bullet wounds."[72]

Returning Black veterans' refusal to stop wearing their uniforms and their verbal resistance of white maltreatment, even in the face of death, provide a window into the changing racial climate of the country. Other things had changed too. Especially significant was the increase in the literacy rate of the country's young Black men due to their service in the military. Once conscripted and placed at the military training facilities, many Black men who had never been able to receive an education before were required to learn to read and write in the Army. These classes were mandatory and, according to historian Chad Williams, "the YMCA conducted approximately two hundred monthly lectures, attended by some ninety thousand black soldiers."[73] The thousands of Black men who had benefited from this education were now capable of reading newspapers like the *Negro World*. They could write to their loved ones, and they could also write to W.E.B. Du Bois and the NAACP about the atrocities they suffered in the military—and they did so often. Participation in these types of programs during World War I lifted the dark veil of illiteracy from thousands of former sharecroppers and laborers. This reality became a major factor in how Blacks reacted during the war as well as upon their return home and significantly increased readership of the *Negro World*, which in turn aided in increasing the numbers of Blacks who supported the Garvey movement.

Having stared death in the face in France, Black veterans no longer feared it so much at home. When they returned, they were often ready to meet racial oppression on different terms. Garvey and Garveyism offered many a new option. His rhetoric and electric speaking style fanned the flames that had been kindled in battle and now burned in the hearts of Black veterans.

Garvey himself trusted and respected veterans, and he referred to them often in his speeches. So it comes as no coincidence that Garvey's program, in many ways, emulated the organizational style of the Army during World War I. For example, components of the UNIA included a flag and a national anthem, as well as military-style units like the African Legion, a paramilitary group that dressed in uniform and carried arms. As his organization became more popular, Garvey often used members of the African Legion as bodyguards wherever he went. There were also the Black Cross nurses, a nursing organization based on the American Red Cross. Black women nurses during World War I had often been frustrated in their efforts to join the Red Cross; the Black Cross nurses gave women in the Garvey movement a way to exhibit leadership and to participate in the organization. The appeal of these special units was a powerful attraction for Blacks, who for generations had been barred from such work and subjected to racist stereotypes and degradation at the hands of a dominant white culture.

The way that he organized these various divisions, as well as the fact that so many returning soldiers found a place in the movement upon their return, are evidence that Garvey himself was supportive of and strongly admired by many returning Black soldiers. However, sometimes Garvey's affection for returning soldiers worked against him, as seen in the career of James Wormley Jones from 1905 to 1923. Jones began as a policeman in 1905 in Washington, DC and later moved up the ranks to detective. He joined the military in 1917 and was awarded the title of captain in the 368th division. In 1919, under the supervision of a young J. Edgar Hoover, the Bureau of Investigation (BOI) hired Jones as its first Black investigator in order to monitor Black radical activity. Since whites were not permitted to attend Garvey meetings in New York City, the BOI needed a Black secret agent to infiltrate the Garvey movement and report back to the government. Jones became known as Agent 800. Garvey welcomed Jones into the organization with open arms and became close friends with him. He not only allowed Jones access to UNIA correspondence, but he also made Jones his personal confidant and even gave him the position of Adjutant General of the African Legion.

As a result, Hoover and Agent 800 would eventually destroy the Garvey movement from within. Ironically, without Agent 800, we would know relatively little about the inner workings of the UNIA today.

World War I was in many ways a catalyst of the Garvey movement. The loss of civil rights after Reconstruction and the establishment of the Jim Crow system worked to create extreme tensions between Blacks and whites throughout the United States. In the Caribbean, the frustrations and disappointment of fighting for the British Empire and then returning home only to receive maltreatment with no reward was disheartening for Black colonial subjects. These pressures, coupled with the inability to secure employment or receive a livable wage when employed, further eroded Black-white relations throughout the Caribbean. Finally, the training and international exposure to a larger Black diaspora who experienced a shared condition as well as the literacy education received in World War I combined with Garvey's "defend yourself at all costs" rhetoric awaiting them upon their return worked together with the disappointment and frustration to create an environment in which many Blacks were willing to answer the indignities of racial oppression with new strategies. Most importantly, these combined factors propelled Blacks towards Garveyism.

This World War I context provides the foundation for the Garvey movement. It determined the form Garveyism took in the American West to a large degree. The great urban Black migration that followed the war saw millions of Blacks leave the South for less dangerous and hostile locations. Many chose to move North but some also came West, and they brought their New Negro attitudes with them. Unlike the North, however, the West had already an established nonwhite and non-Black population. Indigenous Americans, East Indians, Mexicans, and Asians permeated the cities and towns throughout the West, where these groups also experienced white racial oppression. It would be in the American West that Black nationalism would come to intersect with Mexican nationalism, East Indian nationalism, and Japanese nationalism, making the West a unique and interesting place, a place where Black nationalism would become multiracial nationalism.

NATIONALISMS

L ike all social movements, Garveyism did not exist in a vacuum. The individuals who worked closely within and alongside the Garvey movement were powerfully influenced by larger world events. Why Garveyites on the West Coast would need or want to work with non-Black individuals or organizations cannot be understood without some knowledge of the experiences of those other non-Black groups. The rise of Garveyism represented one strand in the rise of the colored peoples of the world and their desire to overthrow white supremacy during the World War I era. Many of these groups migrated to places like California, Oregon, and Washington in order to find work and escape their own oppressive circumstances. It was in places like San Francisco, Los Angeles, Portland, and Seattle that these groups converged, regrouped, and found common ground. Yet their experiences in dealing with racism and with other groups of color in the United States were fluid and constantly changing. At times they competed bitterly for employment in the lowest-paying jobs to which workers of color were relegated. At other times, they worked together to protest policies like the Alien Land Laws, which barred Asian immigrants from owning property. At no time did all people of color work harmoniously to support a common cause. This chapter will focus on those brief but important moments of solidarity among the Black Garveyites and the other nonwhite racial and ethnic groups and explore how circumstances in the West, where the existence of large immigrant populations of color, combined with a numerically small Black population, made the Garvey movement unique.

As Garveyism rose in popularity in the East, East Indian and Japanese nationalism rose simultaneously in the West. In San Francisco, Indian nationalists formed the Ghadar Party in an effort to organize opposition to English colonialism in India. Concurrently, Japanese Americans mobilized throughout California to fight the Alien Land Laws and restrictions on immigration. Mexican immigrants fleeing political turmoil in Mexico and their Mexican American counterparts became another potential ally of Black nationalists. In response, the white population spawned racist organizations such as the Oriental Exclusion League and the Asiatic Exclusion League; these groups rushed to join preexisting racist organizations such as the Ku Klux Klan. Such organizations ramped up activities that targeted populations of color while the American government simultaneously restricted immigration and put incoming Indian and Japanese immigrants under surveillance, at times stimulating these groups of color to find common ground with American Blacks. Nowhere was this more apparent than on the West Coast.

However, in order to examine the interracial aspects of Garveyism in the West, an overview of Black migrations to the West should be established. Despite the presence of some Blacks in the western movement of the nineteenth century, the Black western population was always relatively small when compared to that of the South and East. In the early twentieth century a growing number of Blacks moved into the West from the South, seeking to escape the same racial hostility that was driving the larger and better-known urban migration of Blacks to cities like New York and Chicago. While the western migration was much smaller in size, its impact on the West and on the form that movements like Garveyism took in the West was dramatic.

Figures from the 1920 census show 15,579 Blacks in Los Angeles, 5,489 in Oakland, 1,556 in Portland, Oregon, 2,414 in San Francisco, and 2,894 in Seattle.[1] These numbers represented small percentages in comparison with the total population of these areas. For example, Blacks in Seattle accounted for only 0.9 percent of the population.[2] Most Blacks migrating from the South moved North rather than West. The North represented "freedom" from white oppression and the slave-like conditions that still existed in the South. Geographically, the trip North was more accessible as well whereas the West was more distant and life there was less known or understood for most southern Black populations. Economically, there was more opportunity for employment in the North. The West offered no comparatively magnetic industrial opportunities. Finally, there were already large numbers of southern Blacks settled in the northern cities, so the presence of preexisting support systems made northern migration more logical and convenient for many southern Blacks. When Blacks did trickle into the far West, it was primarily through the railroad industry that word of more favorable conditions and employment opportunities there traveled back to the South and East.

One of those employment opportunities that presented itself to Blacks in the West was through the railroad industry itself. Until the golden spike joined the eastern and western railroads in Utah Territory in 1869, the nation's rails had only gone as far as the Midwest. Other than by wagon, horseback, or walking across the continent, travelling from California to New York required a steamboat along the Pacific coast to San Juan del Sur, in Nicaragua or to Panama. Passengers then were transported by mule or rail (in the case of Panama) to the eastern coast of these countries where they could sail by steamship to New York; the journey could take four weeks or longer.[3]

After 1869, as Americans traveled the railroads across the country, it took only four days to go from one coast to the other. Still, the ride could be uncomfortable and tedious. Anticipating a desire for more pleasant travel conditions, even before the transcontinental railroad finally became a reality in 1869, George Pullman had created the Pullman Company in 1862. Pullman saw the opportunity to make millions by creating sleeping cars, allowing passengers to travel in relative luxury. During the day, passengers sat in beautifully adorned seats that folded away at night to reveal comfortable beds covered in the type of fine linens normally reserved for the best hotels. According to biographer Jervis Anderson, the typical train was "equipped with a compartment buffet sleeping car, a drawing room sleeping car, reclining chair car, and a combination coach and smoking car. The smoking room of the buffet car [was] finished in African vermilion wood of exquisite grain, relieved by embossed gold-leather panels and frieze, with carpeted floor and finely decorated ceiling to match. A fire-jet gas chandelier of deflecting mirrors accentuate[d] the silk draperies and vermilion gold finish."[4]

To complete his highly romanticized vision of white wealth and comfort, Pullman hired Black porters to serve white passengers. Having grown up in the slave era, he believed Blacks were especially well suited for service and domestic work and he wanted to reproduce the fantasy of the Southern white gentleman and woman doted upon by congenial Black servants. Black Pullman porters were primarily forced to hustle for tips, which was the only way to supplement their low wages. They worked around the clock—400 hours and 11,000 miles per month—shining shoes, carrying luggage, turning down beds, and often suffering abuse from white passengers. In continuation of the slavery tradition of refusing to recognize the individual humanity of Black men, white passengers called all porters "George," after their company "master" George Pullman.

The Pullman Company became the largest employer of Black workers in the early twentieth century.[5] As Pullman porters set up residence in the towns and cities along the rails, the small Black communities rose up throughout the American West.[6] It was through these Black rail workers and, to a lesser degree, Black shipyard and Merchant Marine workers, that word of the West spread to Black communities in the South and North. It was also in the first decades of the twentieth century that Garveyism and his *Negro World* spread to the far West on the rails and ships.[7] It should be noted that although they represented the most significant labor force as porters, Blacks were not the only group of color to work for the Pullman Company. In the West, where Black populations were not as plentiful, Japanese, Filipino, and Chinese worked as porters as well as in other labor capacities for the company. In the Southwest and in Mexico, hundreds of Mexicans worked as Pullman porters and even held significant power as labor agitators during times of unrest.[8]

In the early decades of the twentieth century, 1.3 million people, including whites, migrated out of the South seeking better employment opportunities in the North and West.[9] Although southern work was primarily agricultural, most whites who migrated were not farmers but blue-collar workers. They headed west to work in the oil fields, the lumber companies, and other industries as cities in the West expanded.[10] Rich whites looking to purchase land also went west. The boll weevil, which was decimating southern cotton plantations, drove some wealthy planters to seek new agricultural spaces outside of the South.[11] With these migrating white southerners came their particular ideas about race and the associated practices that maintained white supremacy.

White supremacist practices determined what sort of jobs Blacks could secure as well as where they could shop, stay, or find entertainment. Every facet of restrictive racial policies practiced in other parts of the country could be found in the West as well. For example, real estate redlining policies[12] were prevalent. In Orange County, California, in the 1920s one deed read: "said premises shall not [be] . . . occupied or used by any person or persons other than those of the Caucasian race, provided however, that the foregoing restriction shall not be construed to prohibit keeping domestic servants of any race."[13] Furthermore, public pools, beaches, theaters, and other establishments such as hotels were racially segregated. Although this segregation was not written into law as it was in the American South, there existed an unwritten policy of segregation in many places in the West. There was little that Blacks could do on their own to contest Jim Crow racism in the West because their numbers were so small. In Portland, for example, Black populations were forced to accept racial restrictions in the early twentieth century because their numbers were too small to effectively resist such racial barriers.[14]

In Seattle, Washington, residential segregation enforced by restrictive covenants had become commonplace.[15] In an effort to change their circumstances, Blacks established local chapters of organizations such as the NAACP, the UNIA, the Urban League, and the National Negro Congress.[16] The color line, however, was concerned with more than Black/white relations. Prevailing white oppression considered any individual of color or group as eligible for the special restrictions and discrimination. The immigrant populations from the Pacific Rim like Chinese, Japanese, and other Asians (as well as residents from Mexico) found themselves facing in the West practices of racial injustice and discrimination similar to those faced by the Black population.[17]

Consequently, the struggle for justice and equality for people of color in the West took a different form than in the southern, eastern, and northern parts of the country. More typically, in the West the battle could assume multinational and multiracial forms, as it did when civil rights organizations in the Black community allied themselves on occasion with Asian groups in Seattle.[18]

As Garveyism expanded in the West, Black nationalists would come to rely on Mexican American and Asian collaborators in their efforts against the growing Klan presence in the region. The Klan organized not only against Blacks, but also Jews, Catholics, and immigrants. In San Diego, Klan members worked to block

Mexicans from participating in local political events; indeed, lynching Mexicans as they attempted to cross the border was not uncommon.[19] In the West, the Klan reacted strongly towards Mexicans, whom they perceived as especially dangerous to white supremacy due to their adherence to Catholicism, their indigenous-Spanish heritage, and the perception by Klan members that Mexicans were communists.[20] From 1901 to 1928 there were at least 117 documented lynchings of Mexicans in the American West, though there were probably many more.[21] In Oregon, in 1923, the state legislature worked with the Klan to draft and pass a bill that would bar immigrants, especially Japanese and other Asians, from owning land.[22]

The Klan existed in nearly every western state. In Oregon, Klan membership reached its height in the 1920s. The organization was so prolific in this state that Klan members marched in parades through the streets on a regular basis in full costume while standing on floats and waving to the crowds.[23] According to historian Darrell Millner, in Oregon, a popular pastime was to hold a "mock lynching" in which "the victim would be kidnapped by a group of hooded men, taken to a remote location, have a noose put around their neck, and be hoisted off the ground but lowered before death resulted and then ordered to leave the state."[24] In Washington, the Klan presence was heavy in Seattle and Bellingham. In 1925 the Klan made front-page news as approximately 25,000 assembled in the town of Lynden, just north of Bellingham. It was reported in the *Lynden Tribune* that "The largest crowd that has ever assembled in the Lynden district gathered Saturday evening at the Northwest Washington Fair Grounds to witness the public demonstration of the Ku Klux Klan."[25] Further south in California, the Klan had established itself in small towns like Bakersfield, where the police chief and the magistrate were both Klansmen.[26] It also organized in big cities like San Francisco where Klan members included deputy sheriffs, firemen, policemen, ministers, and public officials.[27] Likewise, it spread to Los Angeles, Sacramento, and towns and counties throughout the state.

Many Blacks who went west after World War I refused to remain in the southern towns in which they lived due to the postwar race riots during the Red Summer of 1919. Later riots—such as the Tulsa race massacre of 1921, which was the largest race riot in American history, spread over thirty-five city blocks, and killed upwards of 300 people—drove Blacks towards the West.[28] As Blacks moved West during and after World War I, some carried the New Negro militancy with them. As in the American South, Garveyism in the West established itself as a counterweight to white supremacist activity in many of the towns and cities where the Klan had a presence,[29] such as in Bakersfield, San Francisco, Los Angeles, Fresno, San Diego, Portland, and others.[30]

The West, which clearly had the same racial problems as the rest of the country (albeit not as violent, as deadly, or as institutionally entrenched as in the South), such as the aforementioned Klan presence, housing segregation, and other racist practices, pushed many Blacks towards Garvey's unifying nationalist message. Other racial groups also formed nationalist movements on the West Coast. These groups connected with the Garvey movement at times and in some cases worked in conjunction with Garveyites to address common issues.

The UNIA chapter in Seattle was established in 1919 when Marcus Garvey presented his nationalist vision to a crowd of two hundred Seattleites at the Madison Street Theater.[31] The UNIA in San Diego also formed in 1919. The Los Angeles branch of the UNIA, which became the most profitable and the largest with approximately 1,000 members, formed in 1920. Even though only 2.71 percent of the population in Los Angeles—or 15,579 out of 576,673—was Black in 1920,[32] by the time the UNIA materialized, Los Angeles already exhibited a lively Black cultural life, which boasted a Black YMCA and YWCA, an NAACP, a branch of the National Negro Business League, several Black newspapers, and Black hospitals, hotels, and restaurants.[33] In Los Angeles the UNIA emerged as an important force in local racial affairs.

One reason for its high profile was that the founding group included individuals from the elite strata of Los Angeles' Black leadership. These figures included John Wesley Coleman, a local Black businessman, and J. D. Gordon, a popular Black preacher and the future UNIA assistant president general to Marcus Garvey. Meetings in the Los Angeles UNIA division were held on Central Avenue at the Rev. Gordon's Tabernacle Baptist Church, which hosted a large congregation. Other prominent Black leaders in the UNIA included Joseph and Charlotta Bass,[34] the editors of the *California Eagle*—the most widely read Black newspaper in Los Angeles.

Noah Thompson, the only Black journalist in Los Angeles who worked at a white newspaper, the *Los Angeles Evening Press*, became the local UNIA president.[35] Since the *Evening Press* did not have much interest in the activities of the Black community, Thompson did not write a large number of articles for them. However, he did have a very strong presence in the Black community and often spoke about Black issues to both white and Black audiences. Furthermore, Thompson was good friends with then governor of California Hiram Johnson, who proposed Thompson for the position of United States Minister to Liberia.[36] In his speeches to the Los Angeleno UNIA members, Noah Thompson's rhetoric regarding the desire for unity of all peoples of color was clear. In one such presentation, Thompson stated: "This movement means that every person not white is behind every other person not white, regardless of his standing intellectually, socially, or financially."[37]

The prominence and influential connections of this cadre of Black leaders in Los Angeles stood in contrast to the problematic relationship that Garvey himself had to East Coast elites, both white and Black. They saw Garvey as an outsider and linked him to the lower caste Black masses, rather than to what Du Bois came to call the "Talented Tenth."[38] Charlotta Bass, who worked as Lady President of the Los Angeles women's UNIA chapter for a time, also worked in a leadership position for the NAACP. Noah Thompson, in conjunction with his role as a leader in the UNIA Los Angeles division, was the founding leader of the Los Angeles Urban League. On the East Coast Garvey and his UNIA were bitter enemies of the NAACP and the Urban League, rendering such interorganizational cooperation unthinkable there. Even the locations for meetings differed between the East and West coasts: in Los Angeles, the UNIA and the NAACP held meetings in the same Tabernacle Baptist church.[39]

On one level, the geographical distance between the East Coast UNIA chapters and those on the West Coast created a buffer between the West Coast members and their eastern counterparts. It was also useful to some degree in insulating the West from the power competition that reached intense levels in the East. According to Emory Tolbert, the vitriol exchanged between Black leadership in the Northeast, as found in the communications between Cyril Briggs (leader of the African Blood Brotherhood), A. Philip Randolph and Chandler Owen (editors of *The Messenger*), W.E.B. Du Bois, and others against the UNIA, lost power by the time news of these debates reached Los Angeles and other western urban centers.[40] To further complicate West Coast Garveyism and distinguish it from the East, cities along the West Coast differed significantly from each other in the configuration of their leadership, the strategies they adopted, and the objectives they pursued. Finally, the fact that Garvey himself was located so far from the UNIA's western chapters lessened his personal control over the organization in the region.

One interesting case that highlights the stark contrast between West Coast Garveyism and Garveyism elsewhere is the relationship between J. D. Gordon and his friend John Scott. Scott was a white entrepreneur and Los Angeles Universalist minister; Gordon served as Marcus Garvey's assistant general president. The two had worked together on an Arizona land project in 1921 in which they intended to purchase land and build an all-Black school.[41] Gordon's position as assistant general president motivated him to move from his home and church in Los Angeles to New York City, where he worked at the UNIA headquarters. Gordon was the most powerful of all the UNIA assistant generals. He often took charge of the office and financial matters when Garvey was on tour. From his New York location, Gordon kept in dialogue with his white friend in Los Angeles. Scott very much wanted the UNIA to be involved in his plans for a Tuskegee-like institute that would be created through financial donations from wealthy white philanthropists, with the ultimate goal of establishing autonomous Black agriculturally based townships.[42] Although Gordon could not convince Garvey and the national UNIA leadership to associate itself with this white philanthropist's scheme, Gordon himself privately donated to the project while in his leadership position with the UNIA.[43] This special circumstance highlights how West Coast Garveyites had a more open mind when it came to interracial cooperation, even with whites, than the traditional definition of Black nationalism under Garvey would suggest.

Garveyism continued to spread along the West Coast in small towns and larger cities.[44] West Coast UNIA chapters varied from each other significantly. Economically, in some areas like Los Angeles, divisions between Garveyites and the Black middle class were practically nonexistent.[45] Further north, in Seattle, the only UNIA chapter in the city split along class lines. The first UNIA chapter in the US was organized in 1917, but "by 1924 Seattle had a second UNIA chapter, Division 97. Internal dissention [sic] and class differences probably prompted the formation of the second group, which consisted of two lawyers, a real estate agent, and the owner of the city's only black trucking firm, but virtually no working-class Garveyites."[46] This differed greatly from the lack of class division experienced in the Los Angeles UNIA.

Like those in the Northeast, established Black communities in the Pacific Northwest, eager to maintain an air of dignity and refinement, often resented incoming Black southern migrants who brought with them their unrefined habits. In Oakland, California, the opposite was true. There, the movement reflected working-class issues and circumstances. According to historian Robin Dearmon Jenkins, "[in Oakland], Garveyites built on the labor organizing of Black dining car workers. Fewer than 10,000 African American men lived in the Bay Area in the 1920s, but one third of them were employed by the transcontinental railroads."[47] San Francisco and Oakland were important cosmopolitan cities for Garveyism and other nationalist movements. Together, they constituted a major shipping port that connected the Pacific Coast to Asia, South America, Central America, the West Indies, and the Pacific Islands. The Black communities in these areas included Chinese, Filipino, and Mexican populations, where there was a level of support amongst community members who shared a common foe.[48] In the West, Garveyism grew to maturity alongside other populations of color, all struggling against the same forces of imperialism that had characterized the nineteenth century both globally and in the US. This close proximity and these common enemies predictably worked to create opportunities for collaboration. These interracial collaborations, which will be discussed in greater detail, represent an important difference between Garveyism in the West and Garveyism in other parts of the country.

It would be a mistake, however, to assume that such alliances were automatic, in spite of the common opponent of racism. In fact, there were numerous factors in western nonwhite multiracial relations that functioned to create conflict between the various groups of color. Most of these factors arose around the few economic opportunities available to people of color in a region historically dominated by white supremacist practices. Various groups of color found themselves, in essence, competing against each other for the economic leftovers of the dominant white population. Sizeable Asian populations in the West predated the arrival of a significant Black population. Populations of Mexican descent had an even larger and longer involvement in the West and Southwest than Asians. The potential for conflict among these nonwhite racial groups was evident.

Seattle witnessed such competition in the late nineteenth and early twentieth centuries. The Asian presence there preceded a significant Black presence by two decades, the latter arriving in the city in the 1880s. Chinese laborers had come to Seattle in the 1860s to build railroads and work in nearby mines, among other forms of working-class labor. Later, large numbers of Japanese immigrants moved to Seattle to work in the fishing and agricultural industries, both domestic and commercial. They also worked in the domestic service industry, which was an industry generally relegated to Blacks in other parts of the country. In the early twentieth century, Seattle held the second largest Japanese population in North America after Los Angeles.[49]

The large and established Asian communities could at times create conflict among other groups of color in the labor force. This was particularly true for Black women workers, who had a difficult time in Seattle because they were primarily relegated to domestic service positions. By the 1920s, Japanese and Filipino men as well as Swedish women who migrated to Seattle also began filling these domestic roles, pushing Black women further to the periphery of the workforce.[50] The intergroup of color cooperation that emerged in some western cities in the Garvey movement is all the more consequential because of this economic context of competition for jobs.

Yet, in the early decades of the twentieth century significant global as well as local dynamics worked towards an increase in cooperation among groups of color. For example, following World War I, Blacks in the United States had good reason to support the Japanese on both national and international levels. At the 1919 and 1920 Paris Peace Conference, during which the Allied Powers imposed harsh restrictions on Germany, Japan attempted to add an amendment to the treaty that called for an end to global racial discrimination.

The article for racial equality captured eleven votes of the seventeen possible. Even China, a country in constant conflict with Japan, supported the article. This overwhelming support, however, made no difference to committee chair Woodrow Wilson, who ruled that because the vote was not unanimous, the measure could not pass, even though other initiatives that passed were not approved unanimously.[51] Wilson's opposition was not surprising given that he held conventional Southern white racist views. The willingness of Japan to raise the issue highlighted the increasingly contentious role racial issues would play in the global battles over colonialism in the post–World War I era.

On the national level, Marcus Garvey himself often collaborated with the Japanese from his base in Harlem. However, there were major differences between Garvey's interactions with the Japanese in New York and those between Japanese residents and immigrants and West Coast Garveyites. In New York, Japanese interactions with Garveyism were mostly ideological and theoretical. The primary difference was that most of the Japanese men who met with Garvey were not residents of the United States; therefore, they were not personally subjected to the oppressive racial conditions that Japanese Americans experienced in the West.

In New York, Garvey's economic interest in the Japanese centered on the possibility that Japan could provide financial aid to the UNIA and its Black Star Line (BSL) as well as negotiate a possible trade agreement between his organization and that nation. A major ideological component of the Garvey movement was to establish trade with the colored world in an effort to end reliance on European economic domination of the colored world. In October 1920 it was reported that Garvey met with two Japanese officials in New York for a lengthy discussion of opening trade networks between the UNIA and Japan through the BSL. According to FBI reports, the Japanese officials "had credentials from the premier of Japan" and had "promised to offer their merchandise at prices much lower than what the US could sell, and to convince the Negroes that it would be far more advantageous to throw their lot in with Japan."[52] Japanese delegates were invited to speak at the 1921 UNIA convention in New York City to spur collaboration between the non-European races. Garvey wished to establish a connection with a bank in Japan in order to obtain financial backing for his second attempt at a shipping line. These East Coast interactions between Japanese officials and Garvey himself were for the most part economically motivated business negotiations. In the American West, the interactions between local Garveyites and the resident Japanese living on the West Coast were very different. They were more personal, intimate, and focused on a shared need for social justice.

In the West, Japanese residents, as other groups of color, were forced to live with racial policies that worked to keep them economically depressed. The Garveyites understood that with such small numbers in the West, the Black population would need to lend support to the Japanese residents in order for their own movement to gain momentum. For example, when the Alien Land Act went into effect in California during the early twentieth century, Japanese citizens were prohibited from owning or leasing land. UNIA members in California worked together with Japanese Americans to protest this act. Garveyites in the West were very much aware of the efforts made by Japanese delegates at the Paris Peace Conference and knew that it was the Japanese who had pushed for global racial equality, going so far as to walk away from the table when the amendment was not passed. At a UNIA meeting in Los Angeles, J. D. Gordon "advised his hearers not to countenance or assist the Anti-Alien Land Law and the Anti-Japanese Movement. He said the Japanese are our best friends because they injected into the peace conference the equality of the races, without regard to color."[53]

UNIA divisions in San Francisco were funded by Japanese interests,[54] and UNIA organizers even as far west as Honolulu collected donations from both Japanese and Chinese populations.[55] While these mutual support activities were not successful in reversing the anti-Japanese and anti-Chinese policies, they do stand as evidence of the multiracial and multinational vision of racial progress that flowed between West Coast Garveyites and Asian populations in the era.

An even clearer connection between the strategies of West Coast Garveyites and the growing anti-colonial struggles of the early twentieth century is displayed in the relationships Garveyites forged to demand the end of British colonial domination in India. For Indians to work in conjunction with Black nationalists was not unreasonable: the advent of World War I distracted England from its colonial domination of India, weakening the bonds of control necessary for efficient colonization.

As a result, the Indian anti-colonial movement had increased opportunities for resistance against English domination. Indian nationalist groups organized both within and outside of India, including California as they expanded globally in the hopes of finding asylum in cities and towns outside of India.[56] For the American West, the primary city in which Indian nationalists organized was San Francisco. They entered into US universities and used the press to educate Westerners on the atrocities of British colonialism in India.

The Indian global anti-colonial movement was not limited to intellectual elites. During the nineteenth century, Indian workers had often been utilized as an indentured labor force to replace slave labor in other European colonies as systems of slavery were abolished.[57] This circumstance created resident populations of Indian descent in those colonies and former colonies with a distinct blue-collar orientation. Indian immigration and migration to the American West in the early twentieth century reflected a similar working-class consciousness. For many Indian western residents, there was no escaping the restrictions and discrimination directed at people of color. Resistance to such repression was linked to Indian nationalism.[58]

One example of racism Indians faced was the Asiatic Exclusion League, which was first established in San Francisco in 1906 and moved up the coast to the Pacific Northwest a year later. The Asiatic Exclusion League had formed in reaction to the perceived large numbers of Japanese, Chinese, and other Asian immigrants in California. In the early twentieth century, the Exclusion League soon included Indians in its racial program.[59] It was not long until violence ensued in the form of a race riot targeted at Indian immigrants. In Bellingham, Washington, in 1907, white workers violently attacked Indian laborers employed in the lumber industry. The *Chicago Tribune* reported that the whites were determined to "drive out the 'Hindoos' [as] a mob of 500 white men raided the mills where the [Hindus] were working, battered down doors of lodging houses, and dragged the invaders from their beds, beat them, and drove them from the city limits."[60] The result of this attack was that "six badly beaten Hindoos [were] in the hospital, 400 frightened and half naked Sikhs [were] in jail and the corridors of the city hall, guarded by policemen, and somewhere between Bellingham and the British Columbia lines [were] 750 natives of India, making their way to Canadian territory."[61] The Indian laborers fled to Vancouver, British Columbia, assuming perhaps that since India was a British colony and Canada a British protectorate, they would have protection in the latter nation. On the contrary, responding to rumors that hundreds of Indians were about to descend upon Vancouver, whites there organized and began the largest race riot on Vancouver history.[62]

In reaction to the treatment they received in the United States, Indian laborers in the Pacific Northwest formed the Pacific Coast Hindustan Association (PCHA) in order to address their mistreatment and to organize in the work camps. Through this organizing they began the Ghadar Party, one of the most radical Indian groups outside of the British Empire in the early twentieth century.[63] The Ghadar Party quickly swelled to include Indian students and intellectuals in conjunction with the laborers. Led by Sohan Singh Bhakna, the Ghadar Party organized unity meetings to discuss revolutionary tactics and give anti-colonial speeches in Vancouver, Portland, Seattle, Oxnard, Astoria, and other towns up and down the entire West Coast.[64]

Numerous connections between this emerging Indian militancy and the elements of the Black population comprised an important constituency of the co-emergent Garvey movement.[65] The British West Indies, for example, where Garveyism was born, was also the location of a significant Indian population descended from earlier generations of indentured servants. Because India and the West Indies were both British colonial spaces, these two groups held a shared experience against a common oppression: both Indian and Black groups suffered discriminatory racist practices. Therefore, Indians immigrating to the United States became disillusioned as they experienced the same racist attitudes, such as could be read in an article in the *San Francisco Chronicle*, which determined that Indians should be excluded "because their minds and manners are different from ours. That applies to Hindus even more than to Chinese or Japanese."[66] The emerging Pan-African anti-colonial movement in the early twentieth century was reflected in Garvey's demand to end European control of that continent. The Indian anti-colonial movement found much common ground with West Coast Garveyites, who were fighting a similar enemy in the American racial color line and who saw many parallels to Indian militant nationalism in the Pan-African anti-colonial movement.

Much like the Garvey movement, the Ghadar Party also spread rapidly across continents, and eventually included contingents in the Philippines, Africa, and Central America. Even before the Garvey movement and its *Negro World*, the Ghadar Party members' primary method of ideological expansion lay in the publication of *The Ghadar*, a weekly periodical that printed anti-colonial rhetoric and promoted unity among England's colonial subjects. *The Ghadar* informed its readers that "the paper had reached China, Japan, the Philippines, Hong Kong, Sumatra, Fiji, Java, Singapore, Egypt, Paris, British East Africa, South Africa, South America, Panama, and Trinidad."[67] The Ghadar Party promoted unification of all the colored races of the world and demanded they take a stand against their white oppressors.

In 1913, the Ghadarites created a national tri-colored flag of yellow, red, and green that stood outside their San Francisco headquarters.[68] Four years later, the UNIA created a similar tri-colored flag of black, red, and green. Ghadarites' activities did not stop at proclamations—they also developed an armed self-defense approach to their nationalist agenda. They organized an attack on British colonialists from the shores of San Francisco where thousands of Indians from the United States West Coast, Panama, the Philippines, and China armed themselves and sailed to India, preparing to throw the English colonial government out of their country.[69] As the revolutionaries set sail, Indian intellectuals met in Germany with German officials in the hopes of securing arms and ammunitions.[70] The English were aware of the conspiracy, and thousands of Ghadarites were arrested upon landing and either confined to their homes and villages, imprisoned, or executed. The Ghadar movement reached its peak in the mid-1920s and did not formally disband until after World War II when the goal of freedom from English colonialism was finally achieved.

The British government, which still maintained colonial rule in the West Indies (the birthplace of Garvey), was especially concerned with the possibility of its colonial subjects organizing in the US West,[71] so England reached out to both Canada and the United States to help crush the revolutionaries. Indian anti-colonialists, like the UNIA, came under US government surveillance because these two groups had been observed working together regularly and holding meetings. The US government used this evidence of racial organizing to broaden their own surveillance campaign.

The record of this surveillance shows how Black nationalists and Indian nationalists worked together to organize around a common cause. In San Francisco, a government informant working for the Office of Naval Intelligence while investigating the UNIA met regularly with a UNIA leader named James Farr, whom he described as a Hindu passing as a Black man. Farr, a former bootblack, had put down his brush and polish and devoted his energies to his new position as the President Captain of the Pacific Street UNIA chapter in San Francisco. Farr and another man from India, whose name is listed only as Chatterji, worked closely in an effort to organize across racial lines and incorporate Southeast Asians as well as Pacific Islanders into the Black Nationalist agenda. According to the investigator from the Office of Naval Intelligence, Chatterji was "a Hindu lecturer on politics and on the typical Hindu doctrine of the occult, science, [and] lectures regularly twice a week in the Native Son's Hall on Mason Street, San Francisco. He advertises his lecture topics extensively in advance, especially among the Negroes."[72] Furthermore, the informant professed that Farr and other members of the UNIA had "approached the Hawaiians in this city in order to persuade them to join their colored peoples union plan, which includes not only Negroes, but also all other races other than white. The Hawaiians, who are on the whole very loyal to the United States, are beginning to feel certain racial pride and, coupled with it, racial hatred."[73]

Hindu men passing themselves off as Black was a practice which the investigator seemed to find rampant in San Francisco. He also listed J. J. Adams, the president of the San Francisco UNIA, as a possible culprit, asserting that Adams was challenging to racially define. The informant determined, "his accent was of a negro only by imitation and he was more like a Hindu by real nature." As if the possibility that Indian and Black nationalists were conspiring against the government was not troublesome enough, the events these revolutionaries held at the churches and meeting places in San

Francisco, particularly around Pacific Street, were of grave concern to the informants. One of several popular meeting locations on Pacific Street in San Francisco was the Emmanuel Gospel Mission. Here, the informant noted,

> The music, dancing and the crowd were all very frivolous. The congregation was composed largely of mixed foreign population, Mexicans, Hindus, etc. and a number of negroes. The crowd so gathered could be termed an anti-Caucasian agitation. As a matter of fact, Hendric, a [French speaking] Hindu [and friend of Farr, who also knows a number of Japanese], and a few other Hindus and Negroes were standing outside the door gossiping about their supposed grievances against whites.[74]

The investigator also indicated that he learned "there are several Japanese, such as *Fujii* and *Yoneyama* of the Japanese Central Association who are very friendly toward the Negroes and the Hindus and the Mexicans and planning to organize what they call the 'Colored Peoples' Union,' which will include all the people on earth except whites."[75] According to the investigator, Farr asserted, "[The UNIA] means to and will in time have something to do and something to say about all the colored races." He went on to state that "before the last convention of our Association, we [sent] invitations to China, Japan, India, and all other colored races, but the Japanese were the only ones who accepted the invitation and participated in the convention."[76] Through this interaction between the informant and Farr, as well as the other Black and Indian UNIA leaders, it is clear that the UNIA on the West Coast incorporated other racial groups into its vision.

Another "Hindu" Garveyite, and friend of Farr, named Gutis, often attended the Japanese Buddhist Church on Pine Street. In these settings, the informant reported:

> Both the Hindu and the Negro preach among the Negroes, Hawaiians, Mexicans and Hindus, the doctrine of the supposed necessity of the union of all colored races against the whites. And they also preach:

Assert yourself, fellow-brothers: hit the white man back twice if he hits you: your hitting him is justified because he caused you to do it, etc. And they fortify their doctrine with the rumored success of the Ganti [*sic*] movement in India, the Bolshevik success in Russia, the rise of the Japanese Empire, establishment of the Negro Free State, etc. Their audience is such that it cares little or nothing about the inconsistency of the supposed rise of the colored races against the whites.[77]

It is evident that the potential collaboration between Black nationalist militants like Garveyites in the West and militant nationalists from other groups of color was troubling to both white supremacists in the US and European imperial governments. Yet, in the American West and the Southwest, the group that held the most potentially disruptive power due to both size and location as well as its violent history with the US was the Mexican and Mexican American population.[78] As in the case of their interactions with other people of color and nationalist groups in the West, Garveyites in the West developed complex relationships with both Mexican Americans and the Mexican government itself in pursuit of their objectives. These relationships unfolded against a backdrop of social and political instability in Mexico. With its troubled transnational past and the reality of Mexico's shared border with the US, it was inevitable that Mexico would be drawn into the changing racial dynamics of the war and postwar years with its northern neighbor.

While the Mexican social, economic, and political situation was chaotic in the early twentieth century, the country did possess considerable wealth in natural resources, potential markets, and other economic possibilities like railroads and industrial development. Mexican President Porfirio Díaz adopted policies favorable to opening the Mexican economy to American corporate interests, which quickly rushed to take advantage of the opportunities. Given the exploitative history that already existed between the countries, Diaz's actions incensed many Mexicans and brought anti-American feelings to a boiling point. It also fueled a strong Mexican nationalist sentiment. When political opposition came to Díaz in the form of his political opponent Francisco Madero, Mexico fell into a near constant state of revolution that lasted from 1910 to 1920. This environment, in addition to allowing the emergence of Mexican patriots, also permitted some individuals with more self-serving agendas to rise in power.

Such chaos had international consequences as well. During World War I, for example, Germany attempted to use Mexico's historic animosity towards the US as an opening to create an ally on America's southern border. The German government sent to the Mexican leaders what came to be known as the Zimmermann Telegram. The telegram, a secret communication issued from the German Foreign Office to Mexico in 1917, stated that as soon as the US entry into the war was certain, "we make Mexico a proposal of alliance on the following basis: make war together, make peace together, generous financial support and an understanding on our part that Mexico is to reconquer the lost territory in Texas, New Mexico, and Arizona."[79] Such intrigue by a potential enemy on the US-Mexican border created alarm in the US national government.

More localized elements in Mexico's chaotic landscape generated borderland crises as well. The revolutionary Pancho Villa, whose base of operations was located in the Mexican state of Chihuahua on the border of New Mexico, produced one such calamity that led to a major US military event before the country entered World War I. In March 1916 Villa led an attack on the border town of Columbus, New Mexico, in retaliation for America's support of his adversaries in Mexico. President Woodrow Wilson reacted quickly to the attack and sent General John J. Pershing along with 10,000 soldiers to invade Chihuahua, Mexico.[80] The danger of a second Mexican-American War was real.

This punitive expedition is a powerful example of how elements of race, international events, and domestic histories often intertwined in the complex proceedings of this era. Among the US military expedition was a large contingent of Black soldiers known as the Buffalo Soldiers from their service during the Indian wars of the American West in the late 1800s. Pershing was comfortable in utilizing such soldiers—as a young lieutenant he had been an officer in a Buffalo Soldiers' regiment with the 10th Colored Calvary in the West. Indeed, Pershing's famous nickname "Black Jack" was a legacy from that part of his career. Originally the nickname was the derogatory "Nigger Jack," a reflection of how white officers of all-Black units (the Army was officially segregated at the time) were often looked down upon by fellow white officers. As Pershing's career flourished, the nickname was sanitized. Later, when the US entered World War I, Pershing was appointed to the command of the American expeditionary force to Europe. Among his troops were again a large contingent of Black soldiers, also known as the Buffalo Soldiers.[81]

Americans never captured or even saw Pancho Villa in his New Mexico invasion, but the intrusion of American military forces did stir racial hatred and increase the fervor of Mexican nationalism on both sides of the border. Nevertheless, the incident did not create the strong anti-US nationalism that prevailed in that era among Mexicans and Mexican Americans. Rather, Mexican nationalism had its foundation in the long national history of Mexican complaints against US exploitation. One event in the small Texas–Mexico border town of San Diego in 1915 is illustrative of the depth of anti-US sentiment in the Mexican American population that preceded the Garvey movement. In that year a group of Mexican Americans in San Diego, Texas, drafted what they called the *Plan de San Diego*. The *Plan* was a radical nationalist proposal to retake the Southwest (including California) from the United States and put it back into Mexican hands. In a gesture of racial solidarity against white oppression, the *Plan* included other races of color as beneficiaries. The hope was that Blacks and other people of color would join the plotters in the attempt to reclaim the American West. It also promised to provide separate states for Black Americans seeking economic autonomy as well as reinstate former American Indian lands.[82] It is clear in the *Plan de San Diego* that Mexican nationalists were aware of Black nationalists' hope to establish Black colonies both within the United States and outside of it for the purposes of political-economic independence. However, white Texans responded violently after discovering the plan and killed Mexicans haphazardly without regard to guilt or innocence.[83]

Existing conditions for both Blacks and Mexican Americans in the US at the time encouraged revolutionary thinking by these two groups. The US government took anti-white threats seriously. One secret government agent report declared that should a German war ensue with Mexico, the German Americans living in the United States might rise up and revolt against the US government in support of the Blacks and Mexicans.[84]

It wasn't just US government officials who suspected that Blacks, Mexicans, and Mexican Americans were planning revolts. Many in the American public in 1917 also believed that Mexicans (rarely did they differentiate between Mexican American citizens and Mexican nationals) were conspiring with Germans against the US.[85] As in the Black community in the South, draft evasion in the Mexican community was common. According to historian Thomas Britten, "between June 1917 and June 1918, 59,145 Mexican aliens registered for the draft, 26,114 were called, and 5,794 accepted for service."[86] Because Blacks and Mexicans were military evaders, often both groups received the same treatment at the hand of the government. Soon, the Bureau of Investigation instigated raids on Black and Latino neighborhoods, called "slacker raids."[87] This stigma of Mexicans as "slackers" was perpetuated well into the World War II era.[88]

With its close proximity, immigration to the United States from Mexico was significant: half a million Mexicans crossed the border with permanent visas in the 1920s.[89] Many came to work and live in the agricultural, mining, or transportation sectors, but there were also increasing Mexican American urban populations. As they moved into designated neighborhoods of color, they brought with them their nationalist pride. According to Theodore Vincent, 1920s Mexican American populations were nationalized because of the Mexican Revolution.[90] Furthermore, in urban centers, Mexican American alliances with Garveyites in California may have been strengthened by the close proximity of Mexican American barrios to Black ghettos in urban centers like Los Angeles and San Diego.[91]

Mexican Americans in the United States suffered from redlining and other similar discriminatory policies just as Blacks and Asians did. However, because the Black and Mexican American residents were such close neighbors and—as surveillance reports confirmed—many residents from both groups attended UNIA meetings, it can be assumed that Garveyites in the West were not ignorant of the problems experienced by Mexicans in the United States. Furthermore, as did the Garvey movement and the Ghadar movement, Mexican nationalists utilized the free press to get their agenda out to their constituency. Many of their editorials were in reaction to the Klan's perpetuation of mob violence and lynching Mexicans and Mexican Americans.[92]

In general, UNIA interactions with Mexico and Mexican Americans fell along two lines: one was interactions between Garveyites and the Mexican government, such as in Baja California, Mexico. The other was the relationship between western Garveyites and local resident Mexican American populations. As in the case of their Japanese-Black collaboration, national UNIA interactions were typically framed around large strategic objectives, while West Coast Garveyite dynamics reflected the more interpersonal tactical objectives of contending with local white racism. Although the national objectives typically emphasized strategic large-scale plans while the local chapters focused on community and local social issues, there were times when the objectives of the national headquarters and the local chapters coalesced in one initiative.

The best example of this can be seen in the national UNIA attempt led by a local western UNIA activist to push for the creation of a Black colony in Baja, California. In 1917, Hugh Macbeth Sr., a wealthy Black Los Angeles lawyer and supporter of the Garvey movement, was the driving force behind that potential colony, which he called Little Liberia in reference to Liberia in Africa—which was also the destination for Garvey's proposed Back to Africa movement. Although Macbeth had no intentions of actually living in the colony himself, he saw the potential for an agricultural center that could aid in the push towards Black racial economic independence. He quickly came under investigation for his colony by the Bureau of Investigation when government agents suspected him of forming the community in order to encourage Blacks to dodge the draft during World War I, but this did not deter his plans. He sent a letter to J. D. Gordon requesting funding for the project from the UNIA, to which Gordon replied positively.[93] The Mexican government at least temporarily supported the possibility of trade and cooperation between Black Americans and Mexico. Furthermore, the governor of Baja California, Esteban Cantú Jiménez, hired James Littlejohn, a Black highway and sewer contractor from Los Angeles, to construct roads from Ensenada to Calexico.[94] The Mexican government also hired Macbeth as the Baja highway company's attorney.

Mexican and Garveyite connections were not the only multiracial connections in Mexico. Japanese migrants also wanted to form colonies in Mexico, especially in reaction to the racism they faced in the US West.[95] Japanese entrepreneurs purchased large tracts of land in Mexico in the geographic regions around Tapachula, Chiapas, and the city of Hermosillo in Sonora, Mexico.[96] Although the Japanese were initially disrupted during the Mexican revolution, US government correspondence reported how Japanese residents demonstrated their support of the new Mexican president Álvaro Obregón when they "expressed their sympathy with his administration, and the Mexican people, and with[drew] their claims against the Mexican government for losses incurred on account of the Revolution."[97] Japanese Mexicans believed that the US was exploitative in that country and sided with Mexican nationalists against the US government.

Further north, in California, Black UNIA members and resident Mexican American populations worked less along lines of macroeconomic interest, forming associations around common issues of social oppression. It was in response to these conditions that Black Garveyite leadership urged cooperation amongst groups of color in order to form a united front. In an effort to promote interracial cooperation, Charlotta Bass often reported on Mexican Cultural Nights in her editorials in the *California Eagle*.[98] Bass also regularly invited Mexican Americans to UNIA meetings. The combined impact of the local multiracial circumstances imposed in the West was a significant factor in the nature and duration of Garveyism in the region.

Thus, in the shadow of World War I, Black nationalists on the West Coast worked in conjunction with Asians, Mexicans, and other groups of color to form a united front against their shared experiences of white oppression. This interracial cooperation did not mean that competition did not exist among or within these groups, nor does it suggest that all nationalist groups had identical goals. However, it does add complexity to previous descriptions of Black nationalism as a racially exclusive narrative. Black nationalists in the early twentieth century on the West Coast were few in number and needed the support of other groups to help meet their anti-racism agenda. Similarly, Indian nationalists, Japanese nationalists, Mexican American nationalists, and other groups of color also needed to work with Garveyite Black nationalists in pursuit of their respective visions for justice and equity in the American West.

THE BLACK
STAR LINE

Marcus Garvey is perhaps best known for promoting the recolonization of Africa by the global Black population and the unification of Africa into one country—a country where Garvey himself would be provisional president. That Garvey never stepped foot on the African continent helps account for his naivete in this lofty goal. In the tradition of concentrating on the most negative aspects of this important movement, Garveyism is often explained by historians as a failed "Back to Africa" movement. To see it this way is to misunderstand the movement's primary appeal and the main objectives of its members, which was to gain economic self-sufficiency and independence from whites. For Garveyites, the formation of the Black Star Line (BSL) was the mechanism through which these goals would be achieved.[1] The BSL, a name inspired by a European shipping company, the White Star Line (best known for its two most famous ships, the *Titanic* and her sister ship, the *Britannic*), became an important central focus of the Garvey movement and served as both a symbolic and a tangible manifestation of the dramatic impact of the movement. Established in 1919, the BSL was Garvey's attempt to create a shipping and transportation line that would allow Black Americans to align economically with other populations of color, including those in Japan, Africa, and the Caribbean, to create a separate corporate maritime sphere in which people of color could participate and could predominate.

Within the global circumstances created by World War I, the BSL propelled the Garvey movement to a level of prominence unimaginable in the realm of racial competition prior to this era. To fully comprehend the popularity of the Garvey movement, it is necessary to understand the central role the BSL played in its rise, expansion, and ultimate demise. The UNIA on the West Coast was tied to the fate of the BSL, and the consequences of the shipping line's failure had a direct connection to the deterioration of the West Coast Garvey movement. It should be noted that neither Garvey's BSL, nor his Back to Africa movement, were ideas original to him. In the early nineteenth century, Paul Cuffee, the well-known Black sea captain and abolitionist who worked to colonize Sierra Leone, started a shipping company which he envisioned would also be used to transport Black Americans to Africa. While Cuffee was based in the New England area, eventually the concept of an all-Black shipping line also resonated in the American West. The career of the Reverend Daniel Johnson of San Antonio, Texas, is one such example. In the 1890s, he formed the Afro-American Steamship and Mercantile Company. The idea was to buy inexpensive, second-hand British ships in order to use them to help Black Americans emigrate to Africa. Johnson believed that Blacks, especially those living in the South and Southwest, would jump at the chance to participate in the venture. Just as Garvey would three decades later, Johnson traveled throughout the United States to sell shares of his shipping scheme.[2] However, at ten dollars a share, in the midst of a depression most poor Blacks could not afford the cost of the shares and the company dissolved due to lack of funds.

In 1914, only two years before Garvey moved his UNIA to the United States from Jamaica, Alfred Charles Sam convinced hundreds of Black Americans in Oklahoma and Texas to sell all of their belongings and invest in his steamship venture. Sam was the son of an African Gold Coast chief and wanted to break the monopoly that the British steamship company Elder Dempster[3] had on the West Coast of Africa.[4] He had proposed a shipping company that would pick up cargo from West African ports for shipment to other locations that would also bring Black Americans to West Africa. Sam was able to convince sixty Black Oklahomans to emigrate to the Gold Coast on his steamer, the SS *Liberia*. Although the country welcomed the emigrants, conditions proved unfavorable to the success of the enterprise upon their arrival. Foreigners were not allowed to own land on the Gold Coast, and disease was widespread. To the great disappointment of the other five hundred Black Americans who had hoped to emigrate to West Africa, many of the emigrants became disillusioned with the plan and left. Sam ultimately abandoned the idea.

A year before Garvey announced his plans in 1919 and called for support of the BSL through the sale of shares at five dollars apiece, an East African prince had also attempted to start a Black-owned shipping company. Prince U. Kaba Rega had emigrated from Canada to the United States in 1916 and settled in Louisiana. He founded the African Interland Missionary Society in New Orleans and traveled the South preaching in Black churches and speaking out against lynching. In order to gain support for his venture, he contacted R. R. Moton, who had become the leader of Tuskegee Institute after the death of Booker T. Washington in 1915. Rega wrote to Moton:

> I have plans by which means I will be able to raise a great deal of money from my race for shipping facilities providing that the Government of the United States will grant me privilege of demonstrating the possibilities and opportunities of the resources of Liberia to my people. I believe that within a short time, I can raise money enough from my people for the purchasing of a steam ship for the wage of this Government and to the credit of my race.[5]

Rega, however, was never able to promote his steamship idea to the level that Garvey would later be able to do with the BSL, partly because it was not a component of a broader comprehensive program as Garvey's was.

The difference between these earlier proposals for a Black-owned shipping line and Garvey's BSL plan was that the latter was embedded in a larger attack on the flood of racial superiority propaganda that whites had used to justify their colonization schemes in the pre-World War I era. Garvey's was the first large-scale movement answer to such white propaganda: it offered an alternative vision of world history that placed Blacks at the center of affairs. Garvey's BSL was not just a commercial activity: it was a confirmation that Blacks throughout the world had a glorious history, originating with the first civilizations of Egypt; they were capable of competing economically with whites successfully in their contemporary world. It provided a vision of a future world in which Black subjugation was to be transformed into Black prosperity. It is this aspect of the BSL concept that gave it potency in the Black populations of the era and necessitated the urgency for its destruction by the dominant imperial governments in the United States and Europe.

In the BSL, Garvey's announced vision became the proof many needed to finally believe that Garvey's chosen pathway to racial progress was more than a hollow dream. As such, the success or failure of the line played a critical role in how Garvey and Garveyism would be viewed by the participants in the racial dynamics of national and global commerce in the early decades of the twentieth century. These participants ranged from UNIA supporters to the colonial governments of Europe and America engaged in widespread colonization in the African and Asian worlds to the indigenous populations of those continents that sought to throw off white domination.

To understand the significance of Garvey's announced venture into international commerce via a shipping line in the racial context of the late nineteenth and early twentieth centuries, the critical role international trade and shipping played in the rise to global dominance of Europe and America should be acknowledged. The collision with previously unknown lands in Columbus' attempts to find an ocean route to the Indies in 1492 accelerated European commercial maritime aspirations that relied on wind-driven overseas trade and added to the race for empire in the resource-rich continents of the Americas. Europe, and later white America, parlayed the wealth and power generated by these trading empires into world domination by the nineteenth century. The maritime trade of enslaved Africans to the Americas tightened Europe's grip on the monopoly of maritime commerce. In places like England and the Netherlands, these trading activities in the form of companies like the English East India Company and the Dutch East India Company were the foundation upon which an emerging corporatization of global trade would be built that eventually led to modern global capitalism. The creation of the first ocean-going steamships in the nineteenth century made operations of these global trading networks both more efficient and more essential to the continuation of white European and American global ascendency.

Indeed, it is accurate to conclude that white Manifest Destiny would not have been possible without the presence of white-owned and -operated global shipping enterprises upon which colonial networks of trade, military power, and international politics were dependent. The BSL struck at the very heart of what white colonialism depended upon: the political and economic subordination of groups of color. With the rise of maritime shipping commerce, white-owned shipping companies held a monopoly on global trade and used that power to control industry and construct multinational colonial networks.

Before the outbreak of the First World War, Britain controlled 43 percent of the world's shipping trade. Two major European companies of the era were Elder Dempster, a British shipping company, and the Woermann-Linie, a German line. The second highest profit-making country was Germany, and the United States ranked third.[6] An example of the stranglehold such companies possessed over their colonies can be seen in Elder Dempster, which controlled 90 percent of the West African shipping trade.[7] They did not just control the flow of goods out of Africa and along the African coast; they also dominated the African peoples. As in all colonial locations along the coasts, Britain used African labor in its shipping industry. African seamen and workers were subjected to racial hierarchies under which they were given the lowest jobs in the industry and paid wages from one-third to one-fifth of what whites were paid.[8] A far worse fate met Africans in German colonies.

In the early twentieth century, Germany colonized the territories known as German West Africa (presently Namibia), Togo, and Tanganyika (Tanzania). There, German missionaries and government officials initiated the first genocide of the century by deliberately implementing the slaughter of thousands of Herero and Nama people inhabiting that territory. As part of that process, the Germans built military and labor concentration camps where they tortured the Africans and performed eugenics experiments on captives as well as starved and worked them to death. This genocide of the early twentieth century is almost completely ignored when discussing the precursor to German atrocities in World War II, even though the events are very well documented and photographed. After the First World War, strong interest in the UNIA spread among the Herero peoples in reaction to the treatment they had received by their German colonizers as well as in response to the exploitation from the white South African regime that replaced the Germans. The UNIA inspired African nationalism in Namibia, which by 1922 had nearly 900 dues-paying members.[9]

The German-owned Woermann-Linie benefited greatly from African labor. While most companies working in the region rented African slave labor from the concentration camp officials, the Woermann-Linie was so wealthy they could build their own concentration camp just for the purposes of maintaining their shipping profits. They used two of their own ships to intern Africans in floating concentration camps.[10] Thousands of Africans, primarily women and children, died under the slave labor and concentration camp conditions in this region.

As the primary shipping company in West Africa, the Elder Dempster line also dominated shipping to the Belgian-controlled Congo. In the early twentieth century, colonial governments in Belgian Congo murdered approximately ten million Africans in the race for wealth within the rubber industry.[11] Rubber became a significant resource with the mass production of bicycle tires, car tires, and other major products of the Industrial Revolution. It was E. D. Morel, a clerk for the Elder Dempster Company, who, upon noticing that only guns and chains were being imported into Congo and rubber coming out, quit the company and led the crusade to bring the world's attention to the genocide occurring in the Congo.[12] European domination of the maritime industry was a serious problem for African merchants who attempted to eke out a living in the industry. As a result, the idea of a Black-owned and -operated shipping industry was an attractive alternative. After the First World War, a shift occurred in the shipping industry, potentially rejuvenating the possibility of a new shipping company like the BSL.

One of the many benefits England and the United States gained when Germany crumbled at the end of the war was the division of the German shipping market. In Africa, the displacement of the Woermann-Linie solidified the monopoly of the Elder Dempster company.[13] The war also destroyed much of the shipping industry stock in ships used for trading purposes and opened the maritime trade to less powerful participants. The First World War in effect created a potential opportunity for non-Europeans, such as Japan, to intrude into trading activities previously dominated by whites. Although the United States and England quickly worked to fill in the maritime gap left by the decline of the Woermann-Linie, as we will see, there were notions amongst Blacks, Indians, Chinese, and others of the possibility that this reorganization of the former colonial system could create room for new economic opportunities for the colored world.

The idea of an all-Black-owned shipping line that would sail from the United States and the Caribbean to West Africa created excitement and helped spread awareness of Garveyism throughout the African continent. In Africa, UNIA divisions were created in Nigeria, Sierra Leone, South Africa, and Liberia. In other regions of Africa, such as the Congo, colonial officials greatly feared Garvey's activities. Black missionaries were eventually banned from the Congo because "Belgian officials believed that the ideas of Pan-Africanism found in Garvey's movement had influenced Kimbanguism, Vandism, and other messianic sects that sprang up in the Congo during the 1920s and 1930s."[14]

Kimbanguism, which Simon Kimbangu organized in 1921 in the Congo, was founded on the belief that Kimbangu had received instruction from God to take care of Africans because European missionaries had failed to heed Christ's message. Vandism began in the 1930s as a religious and political movement against the colonial government and its missionary systems. Both movements created intense fear for the Belgian colonial government, who felt movements such as these would diminish the psychological control they believed they had over African populations.

In Southern Rhodesia (present-day Zimbabwe), as in other strictly controlled colonial spaces, a UNIA division was never able to officially materialize.[15] However, this did not preclude Garvey's influence. Garvey's message of Black pride and the idea of Black economic independence greatly inspired Africans even as colonial governments attempted to suppress the spread of Garveyism by banning the *Negro World*. In opposition to such suppression several Garveyite-inspired organizations were founded in this era, including the Benefit Society, which was formed by colonized Zimbabwean workers who had migrated to South Africa for work.[16] Radical organizations such as the Industrial and Commercial Union and the African National Congress of South Africa organized around the rhetoric of Garveyism and, in some cases, Garveyism represented the common thread upon which these organizations connected themselves.[17]

In places like Nigeria, which had large active port cities such as Lagos, it was the BSL that stirred the most excitement for Garveyism. As word of the BSL spread, the wave of momentum for Garvey and the BSL extended far into places that Garvey himself never visited, as attested to by C. D. B. in this article from the *Lagos Weekly Record* (Nigeria):

> An appeal is now being put forth to negroes the world over, particularly West African and West Indian, to give this new line of steamers their whole-hearted support. It is but time we begin to think everything black; this is an age of civilization, advancement, and our bigger and more advanced brothers on the other side are daily showing us the way of acquiring great things through mutual co-operation, unison, and brotherly love; and unless we bestir ourselves, go hand in hand and support them, of a certainty we are doomed to remain in a state of subservience, and subjection another century more.[18]

The enthusiasm over Garveyism in Africa focused almost entirely on the possible success of Garvey's shipping line. Most Africans who were Garveyites had no interest in the idea of a "Back to Africa" scheme and did not welcome a recolonization of Africa by Blacks from other regions of the world. One example of this can be seen in this editorial, published in a Sierra Leone newspaper:

> Just how the American Negroes intend to form their republic in Africa is not made clear (the *Daily Telegraph*'s New York correspondent comments), but there are 15,000,000 of them here and the novelty of the suggestion will inspire liberal contribution for the organization. The average American Negro would [be] utterly lost in Africa. As he has adopted the ways of the white man, and as he is to most inferior of

the African race, the reception accorded him, if he ever returned to the land of his forefathers would be very doubtful.[19]

Another example can be found in this letter to the editor from the *Times of Nigeria*:

> Our Conference was of the opinion that we should give our fullest patronage to the Black Star Line, it being a Negro undertaking and its object being solely for the purpose of facilitating and giving us more and brighter prospects as Africans in our commercial transactions yet we should in no way take any part as loyal subjects of British West Africa in the political aspirations as annunciated in the programme by our Negro brethren in America and beyond the seas outside of the British Empire."[20]

Yet, although the rhetoric of a Back to Africa movement (in which Garvey would be the provisional president of the continent) did not interest many African Garveyites, the notion of Black pride and the idea that Africa is where civilization originated represented important factors in their decision to follow Marcus Garvey. However, nothing excited them more than the BSL because an entrance to the global shipping trade became a tangible economic goal for oppressed populations. The push towards shipping as a method to fight against colonial rule had become a real possibility, as can be seen in the case of India.

Due to the interactions between Indians and Garveyites on the West Coast of the United States, it is worth noting that in the late teens and early twenties, and in conjunction with the rise of the Garvey movement and his BSL, European shipping monopolies heightened nationalist sentiments. In 1919, the same year that Garvey created the BSL and purchased his first ship, Indian nationalists established the first large Indian steamship company in their fight against English colonial rule.[21] For India, the rise of mechanization, particularly in the textile industry, made maritime trade necessary for the growth of the Indian economy. By the early twentieth century, the expansion of industry in India had produced a substantial middle class. However, as in other colonial spaces, the English completely dominated the shipping industry, and Indians came to the realization that without access to international trade and commerce there could be no route to economic independence from colonial domination. As England's attentions turned away from India and towards the home front during World War I, Indian nationalism grew stronger, as did the demands for the political and economic independence of the subcontinent. A shrewd businessman and the leading Indian industrialist of the era, Shri Walchand Hirachand, fought vehemently for Indian shipping rights.[22] He refused to be intimidated by English colonial rulers while inspiring indigenous ship owners through his brand of Indian nationalism. Indeed, "shipping, like no other industry, could develop only under full independence and it was therefore not surprising that practically all Indian ship owners were ardent nationalists."[23] By 1930, among the eleven demands Mahatma Gandhi had submitted to Lord Irwin, Viceroy of British-occupied India,[24] the only industry mentioned was that of shipping—specifically coastal reservation for Indian ships.[25] If the government agreed to his eleven demands, Gandhi would give up his protest through civil disobedience.

In other English colonial regions, such as the Caribbean, local sugar farmers and growers of other agricultural commodities also understood that their lack of access to a shipping line they controlled contributed greatly to their economic dependency. In Central America, US corporations played the role of colonizer when the United Fruit Company (UFC) took over hundreds of thousands of acres to grow bananas in Panama, Costa Rica, and Guatemala, as well as other Central American countries. In places like British Honduras and Guatemala, up to the late nineteenth century, colonial governments financially backed a local steamship line to carry mail and fruit.[26] At the turn of the twentieth century, the transportation of fruit was contracted to a carrier in New Orleans even though they did not have enough cargo space for the quantity of fruit produced. Once the ships were full, rather than allowing other shipping lines to access and transport it, all leftover quantities of fruit were dumped into the ocean, resulting in great financial losses for the farmers.[27] According to historian Mark Moberg, a year after the UFC incorporated in the early twentieth century, it "quietly purchased majority ownership of six steamship lines operating along the Caribbean coast of Central America, dramatically expanding its control of the region's banana trade. In the ensuing years United Fruit would repeatedly undermine all rival steamship lines to emerge as the sole exporter of the colony's bananas."[28]

As it did in India, World War I sparked nationalism and the desire to establish economic control among local growers and laborers in the Caribbean Basin. The war sharply decreased the production and shipping of bananas, sugar, coffee, and other commodities. As a result, thousands of workers were laid off and shipping declined. Furthermore, the UFC, through its employment of primarily Black West Indian workers and implementation of Jim Crow racism (i.e. segregation, substandard living conditions, etc.), as well as its practice of strikebreaking using indigenous labor, had managed to establish rigid racial hierarchies that kept whites at the top, Blacks on the bottom, and local indigenous groups slightly above Blacks.

On April 27, 1919, Marcus Garvey held a UNIA meeting at the Palace Casino in Harlem to announce his plans for the Black Star Line. Members could purchase shares of the BSL for five dollars each with up to 200 shares allowed per individual, and every person who bought shares would own a piece of the venture. Also at the meeting was M. J. Davis, a spy for the US government's Bureau of Investigation. Davis reported that "this was the first meeting for the purpose and something between $7,000 and $8,000 was collected in the form of cash pledges. When they have a certain amount of money they propose to get a charter under the American flag. After the charter has been procured they propose to take the matter up with the Japanese bankers and get financial backing from them."[29] In June of 1919, Garvey printed an editorial in his *Negro World*, stating:

> The Universal Negro Improvement Association is determined to lift the American Negro, the African Negro, the West Indian, South and Central American and Canadian Negroes to a higher plane of economic independence, and to this effort every man and woman of color should lend support. Let us all unite and make the "Black Star Line" a huge success, thereby demonstrating the ability of the Negro in this age of reconstruction to in some way take care of himself.[30]

This news of the BSL traveled across the country rapidly. Indeed, even before many western division branches were established, word of the Black Star Line reached the far West through issues of the *Negro World* that circulated along the West Coast.[31] An all-Black-owned and -operated shipping line like Garvey's BSL was a welcomed notion in this region, and the timing of the coming of the BSL onto the global stage could not have been more perfect.

Shipbuilding and the maritime industry represented a central component of the Black labor force on the West Coast. Therefore, the notion of an all-Black shipping line would become the centerpiece for a heightened interest in joining the UNIA. West Coast cities like Los Angeles, which donated large sums to the UNIA through its membership, would come to rely on the BSL as an opportunity for Blacks to participate in the commercial activities of maritime trade. The success or failure of the BSL was of the utmost importance to UNIA organizations in the West, especially in the port cities of Los Angeles, San Francisco, Seattle, and Portland. It would be the realization that the BSL was failing that would ultimately cause the splintering of the Los Angeles UNIA.

In the early twentieth century on the American West Coast, shipbuilding was an economic profit center to coastal cities like San Diego, San Francisco and the Bay Area, and Seattle. According to historian Quintard Taylor, before the war ended, "Seattle shipyards employed nearly 35,000 workers and produced 26 percent of all ships built in the United States during the conflict."[32] Thus, especially on the American West Coast, local economies were closely tied to maritime activities. For Blacks in these communities maritime trades, shipbuilding and related activities came to represent an important sphere of labor and economic activity. Consistent with the racial conventions of the era and in the context of the emerging white labor movements that generally adopted the anti-Black policies supporting white supremacist theories prevalent at the time, the activities of Black laborers in the maritime-related developments of the era were complex, dynamic, and often characterized by targeted working-class white violence. White ship owners and managers played races against each other in these labor struggles. Rejected as potential partners by white labor, Blacks often had few options but to serve as strikebreakers to the advantage of white ownership.

This, in turn, increased the hostility of white labor towards Black labor. After World War I, strikes broke out in Seattle and the Bay Area among unionized white ship workers who demanded better pay and a shorter workday. Blacks, however, were not admitted into many of the labor unions and had no recourse for their own labor grievances. Consequently, when whites went on strike it provided opportunities for Blacks to claim the abandoned jobs. As a result, Black shipyard workers frequently took the opportunity presented to them and accepted work as strikebreakers.[33]

In San Francisco, it was well known in Black communities that racial discrimination in hiring was the norm. One Black man, after arriving in San Francisco, stated, "I had been around here long enough then to realize there wasn't much work Negroes could get . . . Black workers could either go down to the sea in ships or work on the railroads."[34] In the Bay Area it was the presence of the Black laborers, who were not allowed membership in most unions, that enabled shipping corporations to remain in business as white laborers struck.[35] In 1919, at one San Francisco shipping corporation, there were nearly 250 non-union Black workers employed to take over where white union members had engaged in striking.[36] In response to the strikes of 1901, 1916, 1919, and 1920, shipping firms all used Black strikebreakers and as a result were able to profit in spite of ongoing labor disputes.[37] Black maritime workers mobilized around Garveyism's Black unity rhetoric. Garveyites collaborated with Black laborers at the rallies in the Bay Area and the outlying suburban neighborhoods.[38]

In addition to local Black labor, management in San Francisco introduced foreign-born West Indian Black laborers to supplement their local strikebreaking forces. West Indians were brought from Jamaica and settled under guard on ships,[39] such as the "USS *Pensacola*, which was anchored in the [San Francisco] bay, [and] was home for several foreign-born Blacks, principally from the West Indies and the Canary Islands."[40] This combustible mix of labor strife, anti-Black unionism, white management's manipulation of Black strikebreakers, and the importation of West Indian labor in the West Coast ports created a climate ripe for Garvey's program. As a potential new Black player in the maritime world of race relations, commercial competition, and international commerce, the BSL was bound to have a dramatic impact on maritime trade—should it succeed. By the 1920s, Black laborers in the Bay Area were holding mass protest rallies in conjunction with Black railroad workers, organizing around the program of Garveyism to demand union jobs for Black workers.[41] In 1921 a UNIA chapter in the Bay Area was established.[42] In this conflict-rattled environment, the prospect of the BSL held out hope to Blacks that they were destined to be players and no longer mere pawns in the high-stakes game of international maritime affairs.

Unrest on the docks of San Francisco and Oakland during the First World War era was not an aberration. In other West Coast cities, labor strife and racial turmoil were also evident. Specific circumstances varied from place to place, but the fact that many western

Black workers were employed in the maritime industry provided the opening for Garvey's envisioned BSL to have a major impact on Black consciousness in the West.

Seattle represents an example of how the specific details of Black labor and union activism could diverge from the Bay Area–San Francisco–Oakland model while still revealing the power of Black labor in matters of shipping and commerce. In the Seattle of the early twentieth century, shipping was a primary industry.[43] In 1919 a general strike broke out throughout the shipyards of Seattle. Unlike in San Francisco and Oakland, Black workers were not utilized as strikebreakers, but were included in those out on strike. According to historian Dana Frank, "Among those striking were 300 African-American men who belonged to the longshoremen's union, and members of the Japanese immigrant community's independent unions."[44] The reality that Blacks and Japanese were both admitted into the American Federation of Labor locals in Seattle did not mean, however, that they did not have to endure significant hostility or contend with strong discriminatory elements in the labor movement there. For example, "many of the striking unions endorsed a motion of the Washington State Federation of Labor advocating exclusion of Asians from the US and in 1921 supported the passage of the state's alien land law, which excluded noncitizens from land ownership, when Asians were not allowed to become citizens."[45]

In addition to Black and Japanese shipyard and dock workers in the West, there was another category of nonwhite laborers there that was ultimately tied to the potential ramifications of a successful BSL. These were Black and Japanese sailors. In this category, Black and Japanese laborers once again found themselves at times on common ground and forging powerful linkages tied to the Garvey movement in the West. In fact, it was often Japanese sailors who spread the word of Garveyism across the seas and into the global labor context. One West Indian Panama Canal worker, for example, claimed that he and his crew were first introduced to Garveyism by Japanese sailors who brought with them copies of Garvey's *Negro World* and dropped them off as they passed through the Canal.[46]

Such connections between the Japanese and Garveyism operated on many levels. In this period when nationalist elements controlling Japan's government were intent on establishing their own sphere of influence in Asia and the Pacific, Japan could aggressively offer itself as the colored alternative to European and American intrusions into those areas, as they did when pursuing an anti-racism platform at the Paris Peace Conference following World War I. Garvey himself was not above playing to this sentiment when he sought to secure special concessions from and establish diplomatic ties between his national UNIA and the Japanese government at his various conventions in Harlem. One example was provided by a government informant who described an "unsuccessful attempt by Japanese nationalists and the UNIA members in Seattle to create a "Colored Peoples' Union" inclusive of all "except the white or Teutonic races."[47]

Fundamentally, the significance of the success or failure of the BSL in the West rested on the adverse conditions that Black men and women suffered as a result of white supremacist policies in the region. The potential for improved economic possibilities due to the successful establishment of the BSL they would have considered as an attractive alternative to the limited opportunities available to them both before and after World War I under the prevailing racism of the era. According to Gerald Horne, before the war, "no Black man was assigned as a sailor, an engineer, a mechanic, carpenter, an electrician or radio worker. A Black worker could only work as a cook, messman, waiter or elsewhere in the steward's department."[48] During the war, Blacks had gained access to these positions and, at war's end, they did not want to lose those opportunities, even as the need for colored seamen and sailors declined.[49] Therefore, the desire to continue using these skills in the shipping industry, and the idea of working for an all-Black shipping company in which they could also own a stake through the purchase of BSL shares, motivated their interest in Garvey's BSL after the war.

There were other reasons that western Black Americans would find a Black-owned and -operated shipping line like the BSL appealing besides opportunities for both greater employment and ownership of stock. Passenger travel was an important counterpoint within maritime commerce. Like most other facilities in the United States in the early twentieth century, travel by steamship was segregated. The humiliation of Jim Crow travel wore heavily on Black passengers, which led them simply to avoid such modes of travel whenever possible. In addition to segregated accommodations on board ships, Black passengers were typically denied access to many shipboard services and subjected to other humiliating experiences en route. All such discrimination was based solely on race and not on considerations of class or economic status. Even Black first-class ticket holders were not allowed to dine until the white passengers were finished with the use of the facilities.[50] But the harshest example of such discrimination was perhaps directed at the family members of Black soldiers who had been killed while defending "democracy" in World War I. Women who lost loved ones in the war were called Gold Star Mothers and it was the policy of the US government to pay for their passage to Europe in order to visit the gravesites of their loved ones. An article of the period in Portland's local Black newspaper, *The Advocate*, stated that after it was discovered that many Black women had applied, "it was decided that the best method to approach the situation, due to the fact that a large number of the white gold star mothers from the Southern states were to make the pilgrimage, was to organize separate groups."[51]

Infuriated with the decision to segregate the passengers by race, Black women determined that they would rather not go at all than to suffer such humiliation aboard the steamships. Letters to the editor of *The Advocate* reflect such indignation. One missive declared, "Despite my intense desire to visit the grave of my beloved husband,

I should feel that I would be offering an insult to his memory and the greatest sacrifice that he has made for his country and his race if I were to accept such a Jim Crow invitation."[52] Another letter stated, "My going on such a pilgrimage would be an insult to my dead son who gave his life for his country's cause."[53] Though these letters were written a few years after the failure of the BSL, they nonetheless capture the anger that Blacks of the period felt when confronted with the Jim Crow humiliation common at the time. The prospect of being able to travel on a Black-owned ship where such affronts would not exist had a powerful appeal to Blacks of all classes and genders. Therefore, when Garvey proposed his BSL in this racially-defined environment, it appealed to Blacks not just for economic reasons but for emotional and psychological reasons as well.

Excitement and support of the line on the West Coast can be seen in the funds that wealthy UNIA members donated in 1921 as well as in the rapid rise in the purchase of BSL shares by low-income supporters. As part of his effort to raise twenty thousand dollars for the BSL in California, Vice President-General of the UNIA J. D. Gordon "spoke at a meeting of negroes April 17th in Los Angeles. About 1800 were present. 125 new members were enrolled in the Local UNIA and has raised between 3 and 5 thousand dollars."[54]

Clearly, many Blacks of the era felt that it was not entirely unlikely that an all-Black shipping line could succeed, given the global circumstances in the shipping industry at the end of World War I. The BSL could potentially pose a real threat to European global commercial dominance in theory, if not in practice. Whites in Europe and America understood this potential and took it seriously. Concurrently, colonized populations also understood the commercial dynamics of the post–World War I environment and sought to take advantage of them to reverse white colonization of the colored world, an effort that would in many ways define the twentieth century.

Support for the BSL from the colonized world spread quickly. By May of 1920, according to Tony Martin, there were BSL shipping offices "in New York, Cuba, British Guiana, Haiti, Jamaica, Bocas del Toro, Port Limon, Lagos, Monrovia (Liberia), Sierra Leone, and fifteen other states in the United States."[55] In those places where the BSL took root, the colonial governments and the US government took the potential threat they perceived the BSL to be seriously and reacted accordingly. For example, the "British administration in Dominica passed a law aimed specifically at BSL stockholders, against the remittance overseas of more than ten dollars in a fortnight."[56] And communications to BSL offices from the Congo "were intercepted and destroyed."[57]

It is widely asserted among Garvey historians that Garvey's mismanagement of the BSL contributed to the downfall of the enterprise. According to Ula Taylor, "mismanagement of the Black Star Line gave the US government legal justification to entangle Garvey in a web of innuendo and fraud."[58] Another scholar stated that "UNIA members bought stock in a company but lost their investments due to mismanagement and poor business decisions by Garvey's hirelings."[59] And Adam Ewing suggested that "despite repeated assurances to the contrary, the finances of the Black Star Line were in ruin, the impressive fundraising tallies overwhelmed by mismanagement, inexperience, and graft."[60] None of these assertions are inaccurate. Garvey and his organization made many mistakes in the management of the BSL. Yet, such allegations do not tell the whole story. The failure of the BSL was not merely the product of Garvey's mismanagement. White business interests, as well as US and colonial governments, sought to undercut emerging challenges from people of color to their domination of global commerce in the post–World War I era. Just as Blacks in the West could conceive of the benefits that an enterprise like the BSL could mean for their future prospects in matters both racial and economic, other western populations of color could appreciate this opportunity for their

own nationalist objectives. When such groups attempted to organize along similar plans as the BSL, they too felt the weight of white
opposition that was a large part of the reason for the ultimate failure
of the BSL. The failure of these similar nonwhite maritime enterprises in the period offered another arena in which people of color
in the West witnessed the similarities of their racial circumstances.
Such recognition contributed to the awareness that motivated the
interracial alliances with Black Garveyites as a possible avenue to
mutual progress.

In the West, this dynamic can perhaps best be seen in the example
of the attempt by San Francisco–based Chinese Americans to form
their own trans-Pacific shipping company circa 1915. When the
white-owned Pacific Mail Steamship Company went out of business at that time, the Chinese business community in San Francisco
attempted to fill the vacuum by initiating the China Mail Steamship
Company (CMSS). American corporations moved quickly to buy
up the ships formerly used by the defunct Pacific Mail Steamship
Co., leaving available for the CMSS only one rickety ship, the SS
China. Building a successful business on such a shaky foundation
was highly unlikely; however, as in the case of the initial enthusiasm of Black investors in the BSL, and undoubtedly for similar psychological reasons, Chinese and Chinese Americans jumped at the
opportunity to support the CMSS.

One Chinese Hawaiian wrote: "We are very happy to learn
that you have purchased the *China* and that you have set a date for
its sailing to Hong Kong, with a stop in Honolulu. We are all so
pleased to read this news. Please verify the date of arrival so that the
passengers that we have will be gathered and ready."[61] Eventually the
CMSS would own three ships, as had the BSL, and also suffer the
ills of undercapitalization that plagued the BSL. A hostile govern-
ing body, such as the creation of the United States Shipping Board
(USSB)[62] in 1917, added to its troubles by ensuring the CMSS could
not expand its fleet of ships further since the USSB did not consider

the owners of the CMSS to be "real Americans."[63] After only eight years, the CMSS was out of business.

Like the CMSS, the BSL would also eventually acquire three ships: the *Yarmouth* (renamed the *Frederick Douglass*), the SS *Shadyside* (a Hudson River excursion boat), and a steam yacht, the *Kanawha* (renamed the SS *Antonio Maceo*). From the very start the government worked to dismantle the BSL and the UNIA leadership in general. In one document sent between government officials, it was proclaimed that Garvey "founded the Black Star Line to further dislocate the labor market by inducing Negroes to return to Africa. He also entertains visions and hopes for smuggling shipping arms to Liberia and other African points for the purpose of 'freeing Africa.'"[64] One tactic employed by the government to bring the enterprise to an end was perpetrated through an immediate audit of the UNIA. The audit revealed that the organization used BSL investments to pay for non-BSL salaries and businesses. As a consequence, Edwin P. Kilroe, the New York County assistant attorney, ordered that the BSL incorporate and purchase ships by June 1919 or return all BSL donations to the contributors.[65]

The pressure to raise enough money to make a ship purchase placed Garvey in a difficult position, and this was one factor in the acquisition of the dilapidated *Yarmouth*. As a result of Kilroe's stipulations, having only just announced the creation of the BSL in April, the UNIA was forced to sell shares of the BSL as quickly as possible in order to raise enough funds to make a down payment by June. There was no time to shop around for better offers. The first purchase of the BSL had to be the *Yarmouth*, an aging and rickety thirty-year-old ship that had once been used to transport cotton and coal during World War I. Late on the initial deadline, Garvey did not conclude its purchase until September 19, 1919, for an overpriced sum of $165,000.[66] Garvey unofficially renamed the ship the *Frederick Douglass* after the leading Black political figure of the nineteenth century and made it the symbol of the BSL's arrival on the global scene.

The man who facilitated the acquisition of the *Yarmouth* for Garvey was Joshua Cockburn, a Black West Indian from the Bahamas. Cockburn was recognized as one of the few Black sea captains in the US at the time. The office of the Governor-General of French West Africa described him as "an American black said to have been a captain of a Nigerian Government dredger and later captain of one of the motorboats of Elder Dempster Company's local fleet."[67] Later, it was discovered that Cockburn, through his backdoor deal with the owner of the *Yarmouth*, received a brokerage fee of $1,600 while at the same time acting as Garvey's agent in the transaction.[68] Cockburn would later claim he accepted this fee because he had not yet been paid by Garvey.[69] The bigger problem was that Cockburn was not qualified to negotiate ship sales, nor was he qualified to determine ship quality. He should never have been entrusted with this role by Garvey. It must always be kept in mind, however, that most Black-owned businesses in the United States in the early 1920s faced problems that white-owned businesses did not have to contend with. In Garvey's defense, he may have felt compelled to rely on Cockburn for the transaction, as most shipping brokers and ship inspectors were white and were probably, from Garvey's viewpoint, not to be trusted. In addition, many of the qualified whites refused to work with a Black like Garvey. One such example can be seen in the white nautical ship engineer who was originally approached to consult on the ship inspection, but who refused to work with the UNIA.[70]

By the end of August, in 1921, the *Yarmouth* was no longer seaworthy. The old ship only managed to make three voyages for the BSL before it sank. The first voyage was from the 135th Street pier in Harlem, where thousands gathered to cheer the ship on and see it set off for the West Indies. It barely got to 23rd street before it needed repairs. When it finally did leave the US, it ran aground on a sandbar off the Bahamas. The ship was forced to stop in Cuba for repairs where its presence excited Cuban citizens and boosted

BSL share sales before it headed to the West Indies (Cuba hosted fifty-two UNIA chapters in the early twentieth century). On its second voyage, which set off the day before prohibition passed, Garvey attempted to make some money by using the *Yarmouth* to transport more than a million dollars in whiskey cargo for the Pan Union Company to Cuba. Garvey agreed to the charter price of $11,000, well below the cost of the transport.[71] According to Hugh Mulzac, chief officer of the *Yarmouth*, "the vessel had been loaded in such haste that in heavy weather off Cape May the cargo had shifted, giving her a heavy starboard list. Part of the cargo had to be jettisoned, and the *Yarmouth* limped back to New York under a Coast Guard escort."[72]

The cargo eventually reached its destination, and the *Yarmouth* returned to the eastern US, only to run aground off the coast of Boston. The voyage was a financial disaster. Garvey was forced to sell the aging ship at auction for a mere $1,625.00.[73] Garvey eventually fired Cockburn, who later testified against him in court. Soon after, Garvey purchased the *General Goethals* (also known as the *Booker T. Washington*) for $100,000, which was christened in 1925. Garvey was forced to hire two white officers to man the ship, although he kept an all-Black crew. This proved to be yet another problem as white officers fought with the Black crew and passengers and attempted to abandon ship on a voyage to Jamaica.[74] Unfortunately, by the time the *Goethals* had left New York, there was little Garvey could do, as he was already in jail for mail fraud.

Even if Garvey had been an excellent business manager, the racist context of the times would have made the success of the BSL a long-shot proposition. While the disruption of traditional shipping dynamics by World War I had meant there would be new opportunity for potential involvement in the industry, those war-related disruptive circumstances had also unleashed a level of turmoil in the industry that even long-standing companies found difficult to master. According to the United States Shipping Board records, the global shipping business was both expensive and complicated. In the white-owned shipping lines, claims against the Shipping Board were numerous and included "damages for alleged wrongful discharge, for withholding pay, personal injuries, and salvage services."[75] Insurance rates in global shipping in 1921 increased "from 100 to 1,000 percent due to theft, pilferage, breakage and nondelivery" where complaints were "particularly numerous with respect to the increase in such losses in the Latin-American export trade." The problems in the industry became so widespread that the Shipping Board, desperate for stricter regulation and accountability, recommended immediate "government action in the direction of remedying the evil."[76] To expect an inexperienced newcomer like Garvey to find success in this environment was unreasonable, not just because of his own shortcomings, but also because of these more complex issues far beyond his control. Thus, for many of the world's Black population, support for the BSL in the beginning was more an act of faith based on emotional and psychological factors than a calculated business proposition.

As the problems of the BSL grew, none of them were evident to the general public in the early stages of the shipping line. To the contrary, the physical acquisition of the *Yarmouth* was seen by Garveyites and potential Garveyites around the world as the fruition of their most fervent hopes and the beginnings of a great success story that would transform the Black global experience. The initial wave of enthusiasm and support that followed overwhelmed Garvey and his movement with public acclaim and economic riches. Though the *Yarmouth* never made any money for Garvey or the UNIA, it became a material symbol of Black longing for economic freedom from whites. News traveled fast and far.

The great majority of funds collected by the UNIA were in BSL share purchases rather than donations. This demonstrated the Black peoples' confidence in the BSL as an economic venture.[77] On a promotional tour for the BSL in 1921, Garvey sailed for Central

America and drew large and fervent crowds. Upon Garvey's departure from Costa Rica, a representative of the United Fruit Company, a large employer of Black labor in Costa Rica, estimated that Garvey collected approximately $30,000 during his visit to that country and asserted that the Black United Fruit employees in Costa Rica were sending about $2,000 a month to Garvey.[78] In Costa Rica Garvey attracted as many as 10,000 supporters to hear him speak, who crowded the streets so densely that many were forced to watch from the tops of cars. According to Garvey biographer Colin Grant, so much money was raised for the BSL that Garvey's wife, Amy Jacques Garvey, "struggled to count [it] whilst her brother, Cleveland, was occupied all day and night writing out shares for the Black Star Line."[79] When Garvey traveled to Colón and Panama City in the Panama Canal Zone, crowds from all directions formed so thickly that they crammed the hall where he spoke. The building, meant to accommodate 800–900 people, could not contain the multitude of people (upwards of 5,000) that overflowed into the streets.[80]

In the West, large sums of money were collected from the ever-expanding UNIA chapter in Los Angeles with the expectation that the ships were still viable. However, where the BSL really struggled was in its failure to keep its promises to its shareholders and in the disappointment it ultimately brought to Black supporters when they attempted to cash in on their investments. In an era when Blacks had few avenues to escape the harsh realities of white racism, the supporters of the BSL literally put their lives in Garvey's hands. One such case involved four Garveyites who fled the racist violence of Oklahoma in 1921 in hopes of salvation through the BSL. There, the worst race riot in American history had occurred in Tulsa. White mobs had invaded Tulsa's Black community, burning buildings and killing Blacks at random. Four Oklahoma Garveyites fled to New York City with the determination to board the BSL bound for new lives in Africa.[81] Having previously purchased shares in the BSL and having full confidence in the rhetoric of Garvey's vision, they saw Africa as a welcome alternative to Oklahoma's racist terrorism. Their reality as described by C. F. Simmons in an article about the Tulsa riot was anything but what they had expected:

> The names of the refugees were Lizzie Johnson, Stella Harris, Josie Gatlin and Claude Harris, all from Okmulgee. They had formed part of a group of eight which had left before the riots began. They told terrible stories of oppression visited upon colored people, said that the practice of peonage was common, and colored farmers were kept always in debt, the planters taking their crops and giving them bare subsistence in return. The refugees said warnings had been distributed weeks and months before the riot, telling colored people they would have to leave Oklahoma before June 1, or suffer the consequences. Being members of that body, they had gone, they said, to the offices of the Negro Improvement Association, Marcus Garvey's organization, where they were told they could not be taken care of, and where, according to their accountants, efforts were made to communicate with Okmulgee to prevent other colored people from coming to New York.[82]

As seen in the above passage, with each incident of disappointment, be it in the US or in Africa, or elsewhere, word of Garvey's inability to follow through on his promises circulated among his followers. Like Garvey's reputation, the ships Garvey had purchased for the BSL also began to fall apart.

Garvey also purchased other ships. One such ship was the *Shadyside*, an excursion boat that took guests up and down the Hudson River in 1920. However, prices ($1.05 per person) proved to be too expensive. When winter came, the *Shadyside* sprang a leak and sank. The other small ship he purchased was a yacht called the *Kanawha*. The *Kanawha* had a series of mishaps revolving around faulty boilers, which cost the UNIA nearly $50,000 in repairs. When Garvey sailed on the vessel to Costa Rica to promote the BSL, the supposedly fixed boilers blew again and Garvey was forced to travel on another, non-BSL-owned ship for the remainder of his trip.[83]

However, it was the UNIA's fourth and final ship, the SS *Phyllis Wheatley*, that led to the downfall of Garvey and his movement. In

November of 1919, according to Cronon, Garvey promised that the ship "would 'be put on the African route and sail between America, Liberia and Sierra Leone, West Africa.'"[84] The SS *Phyllis Wheatley*, originally named the *Orion*, was the culmination of all the problems associated with the BSL. Garvey heavily promoted the ship even before he purchased it, which was in negotiation for over a year. When Garvey advertised shares of the BSL using an image of the *Orion* on a postcard, in which someone had scratched out the name *Orion* and painted in the name SS *Phyllis Wheatley*, his enemies pounced on the opportunity to arrest him and charge him with defrauding the mail. At the time, a little-known junior lawyer in the Justice Department was assigned the job of keeping tabs on Garvey: J. Edgar Hoover. The Garvey case was the first career-building move for Hoover as he devoted a lifetime to, in his eyes, protecting America from Black radicalism. Hoover, the man who later in his career would attack Martin Luther King Jr., Malcolm X, the Black Panthers, and many other Black leaders, first learned his tricks in the pursuit and destruction of Marcus Garvey.[85]

In the 1920s, Hoover considered Garvey to be "the most dangerous Black man in America" and he worked diligently to find any illegal activities in the UNIA's various operations to use against him. Finally, in 1922, the Bureau of Investigation succeeded in indicting Garvey for attempting to defraud through the mail when he sent out the advertisement to sell shares of the SS *Phyllis Wheatley*.[86]

Not long after Garvey's indictment in 1923, his enemies, dominated by leadership from the NAACP, drew up and signed a document accusing Garvey of everything from inciting Blacks to rise up against whites and sending his followers to disrupt anti-UNIA rallies to murder. During Garvey's trial, he acted as his own attorney. It was an eventful trial. While the government's case was flawed and the evidence against Garvey was extremely weak, the national racial antagonisms that Garvey symbolized led ultimately to his conviction. Garvey's inept performance as his own attorney did not enhance his chance for exoneration.

After the breakdown of his ships and the trial, the Black Star Line was doomed to failure, but Garvey would not be deterred. While awaiting appeal of his case, Garvey was still determined to keep some version of the once popular BSL afloat. In fact, "while awaiting the outcome of his appeal, in 1924 Garvey organized still another maritime venture, the Black Cross Navigation and Trading Company. Patterned after the defunct Black Star Line, this corporation was chartered to engage in trade between the various Negro areas of the world, and Garvey intended that its vessels would also be used to carry American Negro colonists to Africa."[87]

Garvey was sentenced to five years' imprisonment for mail fraud and sent to the federal prison facility in Atlanta to serve his time. Garvey had a number of health problems, including severe asthma, and he fell ill while in prison. Political considerations related to the 1928 presidential election and the government's unwillingness to elevate Garvey to martyrdom status for Black Americans, should he die in prison, probably contributed to the decision to release and deport him to Jamaica after he served approximately a year and a half of his sentence. The Bureau of Investigation had done what all of his other enemies had been unable to do: remove Marcus Garvey as a voice of leadership in the American Black community.

Over time, the disappointing experiences of Garveyites undercut the faith many had formerly held in Garvey and the BSL. However, such disillusionment was not immediate or universal. Before it set in with full force and the BSL crumbled under the weight of its circumstances and its own shortcomings, Garvey's vision of a Back to Africa movement and the concept of the BSL had a profound and complex impact on the United States, the West Indies, Central America and on Africa, the country of Liberia in particular. Africans especially, entrapped in the strangling web of European colonialism, were desperate for a pathway to anti-colonial freedom and self-determination and the BSL, though short-lived, provided a window of hope in an otherwise desperate situation.

Even the well-regarded Garvey antagonist, W.E.B. Du Bois, recognized the significance a Black steamship company could potentially have in terms of Black economic progress. Du Bois had no faith that such a plan could succeed in the hands of his philosophical enemy, Garvey, advising his uncle, "not to under any circumstances invest any money on the BSL."[88] However, Du Bois did recognize the potential the idea could have if held in more competent hands than those of his archenemy.

In 1923, after the BSL failed, Du Bois wrote a letter to Secretary of State Charles Hughes. In his letter, Du Bois wrote "to ask if there is any feasible and legal way by which the United States Government could aid or guide a plan of furnishing at least two ships for the tentative beginning of direct commercial intercourse between America and Liberia."[89] Furthermore, Du Bois suggested that the government step in and make good the thousands of BSL bonds held by the poor Black Americans who had purchased five-dollar shares from Garvey. In fact, as vehemently as Du Bois and Garvey battled in their newspapers and speeches, Du Bois believed the BSL to be the only worthwhile program put forward in the Garvey movement, even though he rarely missed an opportunity to point out Garvey's inability to manage the business.

On the West Coast of the United States, it would be disillusionment with the BSL that would cause the once prominent Los Angeles division to splinter and ultimately leave the Garvey movement. News of the possibility that the ships of the BSL might not even exist caused concern in both Los Angeles and San Diego. By contrast, in other cities, such as San Francisco and Seattle, the troubles of the BSL, though recognized, did not seem to deter the local chapters from their desire to unify against white oppression. For them, it would not be until Garvey's deportation that the local chapters would begin to weaken and dissolve.

4

THE DECLINE
OF GARVEYISM
IN THE WEST

I n 1921, word that the BSL might be in trouble reached
Charlotta Bass, Noah Thompson, and other wealthy elites
in the Los Angeles UNIA leadership circles. They were eager to
find out if the BSL was really in decline and whether their donations to the organization were being wasted. To help alleviate
these concerns, Thompson took a trip to New York in August of
1921 and demanded to see the ships. He stayed in New York for
an entire month, each day asking to see the ships, and each day he
was told he could see them "tomorrow." Tomorrow never came.
Thompson returned to Los Angeles ready to proclaim the BSL a
farce. An article soon appeared on the front page of the *California
Eagle*, stating: "Thompson was sent as a delegate to New York [to
represent the Los Angeles UNIA], they gave Mr. Thompson nigh
unto $1000 and told him to bring back the dope, the real dope,
the truth and nothing but the truth. Instead of more light [the
delegates requesting to see the ships] got a great big roasting when
Mr. Garvey wrote an obscure member attacking Thompson and
failing to give an answer."[1]

In response to articles such as this one, concerned Californians from other cities wrote to Thompson asking him if it was prudent to continue donating to the Garvey movement. One such letter came from Ella Ross Hurston, who wrote, "I am forced to write you, asking if it is wise for a widow-woman who makes her living by working in service and doing a day's work, to continue to make the sacrifice sending $5.00 per month on payment of shares in the Black Star Line. After reading that part of your report, stating that you and many other delegates were unable to see the ships supposed to be owned by said company, I began to think, maybe I had better keep my hard earnings at home, for I have an aged mother to support and I haven't one penny to throw away. So I am writing you for facts in regards to what I have asked you."[2]

After Garvey's failure to prove the ships' existence, large numbers of the UNIA members in Los Angeles decided to split and form their own group. In 1921 the Pacific Coast Negro Improvement Association (PCNIA) was organized. This new group was not initially anti-Garvey. In fact, the PCNIA still considered themselves to be Garveyites, but they no longer wanted to support the UNIA financially. Instead, the PCNIA promoted Black investment in real estate and businesses in the Los Angeles area.[3] The Los Angeles chapter had been a significant contributor of UNIA funds, and Garvey immediately responded to the crisis by writing telegrams to UNIA members in Los Angeles, imploring them to vote Thompson out and return to the fold. In an effort to rectify the situation, East Coast UNIA leaders Henrietta Vinton Davis and James Eason traveled to California in December of 1921 to convince members to remain loyal to Garvey. But Thompson proved too popular, and member faith in the East Coast leadership was not strong enough to keep the group from splintering ultimately. Three quarters of the 1,000 Los Angeles UNIA chapter members chose allegiance to the PCNIA under Thompson. As was reported in the *California Eagle*, "Out of the gigantic organization which had gallantly marched

under the banner of the Hon. Marcus Garvey, there came forth a
new one last Tuesday evening when by a nine-tenths vote the great
Body decided to form a new organization to work under the name
of the Pacific Coast Improvement Association."[4]

Alarmed by the development in the Los Angeles division, Garvey
determined he would make a two-month tour along the West Coast
in an attempt to strengthen his movement in the major West Coast
cities of Seattle, San Francisco, and Oakland, and also to recapture
the support of what was once his most lucrative West Coast branch
in Los Angeles. His visits yielded some initial success. He made a
strong impression in Seattle, where he spoke at Washington Hall on
14th and Fir streets. According to one proud attendee who was ten
years old at the time, "We met [Garvey] at the Union Station, and
all the Black Cross Nurses and the men were all there (in uniform)
to greet him. And I was the little girl that they gave flowers to give
him."[5]

Garvey's trip took him to San Francisco as well, where he was
scheduled to speak at the City Auditorium. This was the first
West Coast city where Garvey met resistance from local police
who attempted to bar him from appearing. In addition, the local
NAACP and their allies in the city's church leadership also wanted
to thwart Garvey's plans to speak. Of his visit there Garvey wrote,
"When I arrived in San Francisco I was met by a delegation from the
Oakland Division, where it appears that for three weeks the local
authorities, the members of the NAACP, and the local preachers
organized to keep me out of that city."[6] Unlike the Los Angeles
division, the San Francisco, Oakland, and Seattle UNIA divisions
were at odds with the NAACP organizations in their respective
cities. In response to the threats from the NAACP and the police
in San Francisco, Garvey worked with the local UNIA lawyers to
obtain an injunction to bar the police commissioner from disrupt-
ing the UNIA meeting.[7] By the time Garvey came to visit in 1922,
word of the trouble with the BSL had already reached San Francisco,

where UNIA leader James Farr, the "Hindu posing as a Black man," reported to an undercover government informant that the UNIA "suffers a great deal of internal trouble."[8]

After speaking in San Francisco, Garvey traveled to nearby Oakland to give two speeches there. In Oakland, the UNIA Liberty Hall on Chester and 8th Street had a history of interracial cooperation where invited speakers from a variety of countries, such as India, China, and others, often spread the message of racial solidarity amongst the colored peoples of the world as a key topic.[9] Although six detectives were planted in his audience and ordered to place Garvey under arrest should he incite violence through his rhetoric,[10] Garvey's visit proved successful and helped to shore up support and unity throughout the city.

From Oakland, Garvey made his way to Los Angeles, where crowds gathered in large numbers to hear him speak at the Trinity Auditorium on Monday night, June 5, 1922, where the police kept a careful watch. Los Angeles was arguably the most important visit on the trip in terms of West Coast finances for the UNIA. According to one government informant who observed the Los Angeles chapter, "Considerable money has been contributed to Marcus Garvey at the New York headquarters. The negro population of Los Angeles has a large number of exceedingly prosperous individuals, and the above organization has been well supported financially." Furthermore, the informant provided insight into the differences in energy between the UNIA and the NAACP membership in the West, stating: "The membership of this organization are a much larger and more enthusiastic group than those of the conservative negro societies that are working alon[g] lines of cooperation with the whites for the uplift of the race."[11]

As Garvey was understandably concerned about the split in the Los Angeles division and the announcement that the intention of the PCNIA was to promote Garvey's ideas but not fund the UNIA in any way, the primary message that night was one of reunification.

Garvey invoked the lessons he felt that Black people should have learned from World War I: during the war the rhetoric from the governments of Europe and America had emphasized the need for the unity of all people under the Western Allies as brothers and sisters in the struggle for democracy. Once the war was won, the peace revealed that the notion of brotherhood had disappeared and the interests of Blacks and other people of color had been sacrificed to the imperial objectives of colonial whites. Garvey called for Blacks everywhere to unite, for "this is what the program means, Unity. We can't afford to fall out and against ourselves because we are all links in the chain."[12] His speech and his presence likely brought some former Garveyites back to the UNIA. Whatever momentum Garvey had built towards the reunification of his West Coast chapters, however, was soon destroyed by an event that occurred on his return trip east. Upon leaving Los Angeles, he eventually made his way to Atlanta, Georgia, where on June 25, 1922, he met secretly with the Imperial Wizard of the Ku Klux Klan, Edward Young Clarke, to explore the formation of an alliance between the two organizations. Once word of this secret meeting leaked to the public, the career of Garvey and his UNIA would never fully recover.[13]

The Klan was a thriving organization with a membership that would reach more than two million in 1924.[14] Although they did not have one united political platform, the organization was immersed in local and national racial politics. In places like Oregon on the West Coast, the Klan was especially strong. Within a year after the arrival of one single Klan promoter in 1921, "Oregon was so firmly in the grasp of the hooded nightriders that the government admitted they controlled the state."[15] In 1925, in a national show of strength, 40,000 Klan members in full hooded regalia marched down Pennsylvania Avenue in Washington, DC. To Garvey, the Klan represented the power that whites maintained in the country and government. Garvey saw many similarities of circumstance between his UNIA and the Klan. He saw himself as the leader of the Black world and the Klan leadership as rulers of the white world. After knowledge of his secret meeting had blown up to a full-scale crisis, Garvey declared—in an attempt to persuade followers to see his point of view—"The attitude of the Universal Negro Improvement Association is in a way similar to the Ku Klux Klan. Whilst the Ku Klux Klan desires to make America absolutely a white man's country, the Universal Negro Improvement Association want to make Africa absolutely a black man's country."[16] Garvey was convinced, and not incorrectly so, that the Invisible Empire was embedded in all areas of government and in nearly every white organization in the country. He believed that by meeting with the Klan some mutually advantageous arrangement might be worked out that would allow both organizations to achieve their main objectives. At the very least, Garvey surmised that an accommodation with the Klan could reduce the potential for racial violence aimed at his southern UNIA membership.[17]

The East Coast NAACP pounced on this meeting and used it as an opportunity to destroy Garvey. Unfortunately, virtually no written evidence is available pertaining to the actual minutes of the Klan meeting. The sparse written evidence utilized by most scholars to access this incident consists of a brief description by telegram provided by Garvey shortly after the meeting, and the various vigorous "defenses" by Garvey that emerged later in his speeches and writings in the *Negro World*. Only Walter White, secretary of the NAACP, claimed to have seen a memorandum of the meeting, which he asserted contained a deal between Garvey and the Klan, under which the Klan would not impede Garvey's efforts to sell stock in a new maritime venture to Southern Blacks in exchange for Garvey's assistance against Black opponents of the Klan like the NAACP.[18] White never produced the document to support his assertions—which, coming as they did from a leader in the NAACP, the alleged target of the deal, can hardly be taken at face value. At present, the telegram provided by Garvey to his supporters stands as the only firsthand evidence of the encounter.

In theory, there were certain surface similarities between Garvey and the Klan that may have looked like potential common ground, but in fact there were too many more areas of philosophical conflict to allow any realistic framework for collaboration. For example, in Garvey's telegram of the meeting he asserted: "He [Edward Young Clarke, Imperial Wizard of the KKK] believes America to be a white country, and also states that the Negro should have a country of his own in Africa. He denied that his organization, since its reorganization, ever officially attacked the Negro."[19] The historic record of the Klan, however, is clear. The Klan was less interested in the departure of Blacks from the US than it was in their submission and subordination. They were more committed to continuing the exploitation of Black labor than to eliminating it through deportation.

Ultimately, the Klan was an unstable, fractionalized organization even at the height of its power and national influence in the 1920s. Internal fighting among Klan leaders, scrambles for personal financial gain, regional animosities, and differing strategies assured that even if Garvey had reached some accommodation with Clarke and the Atlanta Klan, this was no guarantee that a broad-based UNIA/Klan alliance would emerge. A few years after the infamous meeting in 1922, when Garvey was later confined in the Tombs prison in New York following his conviction for mail fraud, he received a death threat from a Klan member refuting in no uncertain terms Clarke's denials that the Klan would ever attack Negroes. The death threat, recently discovered in the Garvey trial records, declared, "Your hide is not worth ten cents whenyou [*sic*] leave the city Prison, and if you are acquittedyour [*sic*] Life won't be worth tens shillings in West Indian money. A man of your type should be tied to a lynching post and lashed to Death. And if it is in our power to do so we will take you from your guards and killyou [*sic*] before their eyes."[20]

Obviously, Imperial Wizard Clarke did not and could not speak for the entire Klan organization. Thus, while there was no real danger to Black America and its leaders that a powerful Klan/ UNIA coalition was being formed, there were compelling circumstances pressuring both Clarke and Garvey in 1922 that made their meeting in Atlanta, if not inevitable, at least understandable.

Furthermore, although the Klan movement held considerable power and had tentacles of support that reached high into the halls of national power, organizations like the young NAACP and its allies were gaining considerable strength in their anti-Klan activities. The Klan did need help, and Garvey's UNIA was in some respects a logical potential ally. In addition to the few compatible philosophical elements the two groups shared, it should be noted that Garvey started his career as a disciple of Booker T. Washington and his accommodationist philosophy. The possibility of helping to mold Garvey into another Washington must have been appealing, not only to the Southern Klan but to a much wider swath of white Americans as well in the early 1920s. If the Klan was seeking to find an opponent to the NAACP, the organization of Booker T. Washington's chief adversary W.E.B. Du Bois, what better place to look than a former Washington disciple like Marcus Garvey, who aggressively advocated separation of the races, and was himself engaged in a bitterly antagonistic feud with W.E.B. Du Bois as well?

However, for American Blacks the Klan was forever and always intimately linked to the worst days and experiences of American racial life. The Klan, with its Civil War and Reconstruction origins, the role it had played in destroying the promise of first freedoms, and its willingness to utilize the most overt forms of terrorism and violence to achieve its objectives, was the ultimate evil on the American racial landscape. Garvey did not understand this fundamental reality. His level of naivete on this point is clear in his initial telegram following the meeting. Garvey stated, "Have this day interviewed Edward Young Clarke, acting Imperial Wizard Knights of the Ku Klux Klan."[21] Later in the telegram Garvey, with evident pride and confidence, reveals he has tendered an invitation to Clarke to speak at his next convention: "He has been invited to speak at forthcoming convention to further assure the race of the stand of the Klan."[22] To Garvey it was an interview; to American Blacks, it was an unfathomable transgression.

Ironically, nearly one hundred years later in 2013, a local chapter of the NAACP itself held a secret meeting with Klan organizers from Montana in an attempt to find common ground and reconciliation. At the meeting Klan member John Abarr was permitted to fill out an application and join the NAACP, but the NAACP chapter leader could not make a similar choice in the reverse because "you have to be white to join the Klan."[23] This meeting was not sanctioned by the national NAACP leadership, but it shows how these superficial similarities in racial rhetoric among incompatible organizations can mislead historically unsophisticated but highly motivated racial activists, as must have been the case with Garvey in 1922.

After his meeting with the Klan, Garvey took his rhetoric even further by withdrawing his support of the Dyer Anti-Lynching Bill, a campaign that represented a massive effort among Black leadership on the East Coast who fought tirelessly but unsuccessfully to make lynching a federal crime. Garvey argued that speaking out against lynching would only lead to more lynching:

> You cannot put over anything in this country that seeks to change the white man's attitude toward you by taking up an offensive attitude toward the white man if you are dependent upon him to pass the measure for your satisfaction. As proof of what I mean: Since the agitation of the National Association for the Advancement of Colored People about the anti-lynching bill more lynchings have occurred in the United States than prior to the agitation of the bill.[24]

This was the final straw for Garvey's enemies. A. Philip Randolph, Chandler Owen, and the NAACP launched a "Garvey Must Go!" campaign in which they gave numerous public speeches and wrote letters to the Bureau of Investigation accusing Garvey of everything from libel to murder.

Chandler Owen went even further in his anti-Garveyism attacks. Owen lived in New York City and was a socialist follower of Black organic intellectuals like Hubert Harrison. He had joined with A. Philip Randolph to write and distribute *The Messenger*, a leading Black newspaper of the era. Later, Owen moved to Chicago, joined the Republican Party, and would help support Randolph in his struggle to form the largest Black union in the nation, the Brotherhood of Sleeping Car Porters.[25]

During the Garvey era, Owen was a very close friend of Charlotta Bass and her husband. Even though the PCNIA had declared itself an allied organization to the UNIA, he saw the newly formed PCNIA as an opportunity to boost his anti-Garvey campaign. Upon hearing of the split and the formation of the PCNIA, Owen flew to Los Angeles in February 1922 to speak to the newly formed organization in hopes of entreating them to ally with his own growing anti-Garvey movement. One part of Owen's strategy of highlighting the differences between Garvey's philosophy and those of the group he was representing took the argument of racial integration to its logical, but highly controversial, end point. Hoping to turn the PCNIA into an anti-Garvey organization, he declared: "We believe in the unconditional intermarriage of races between any sane grown persons who desire to marry without regard to race or color. We would leave no room for doubt. We favor the intermarriage of Negro men with white women, and the intermarriage of white men with Negro women. It is an unpopular view just now just as most scientific views are unpopular at their inception."[26] This rhetoric stood in direct conflict with Garvey's program of racial separation and hardly would have played well with his Klan allies. The fact that Owen felt comfortable speaking to California audiences about this highly sensitive subject as early as the 1920s is revealing of the particular racial circumstances found on the West Coast. Anti-miscegenation laws would exist in California until 1948,[27] and such laws were also present in other western states like Oregon, which had passed an anti-interracial marriage law during the Civil War era that was enforced until 1951.[28]

Probably at least two factors influenced Owen to tread this potentially incendiary and dangerous path of racial rhetoric in his attack on Garvey. For one, in some measure it was a reflection of Owen's radical socialist roots in which nontraditional racial notions were then fashionable as counterpoint to the harsh sexual and racial boundaries erected in capitalist American racial conventions. Second, on a different level he must have felt it would not be offensive to a relatively affluent, self-confident, and assertive audience of western Black leadership to advocate for this ultimate expression of racial equality. That such an audience could exist in California in the 1920s is probably a reflection of the small and relatively non-threatening size of western Black populations and the comparative success some Blacks, both male and female, had been able to achieve in the arenas of finance and political influence in the West in spite of the obstacles faced there by people of color.

Garvey's visit to the West Coast in 1922 signaled the beginning of the end of the PCNIA.[29] Chandler Owen, unable to create his desired rift between the PCNIA and the UNIA when he visited in that year, redirected his efforts and attempted instead to establish a local organization called Friends of Negro Freedom, which was meant to represent an anti-Garvey organization as a counter to the PCNIA. As one of the leaders of the PCNIA, Noah Thompson publicly supported the Friends of Negro Freedom (even though others within leadership did not) and formed a friendly alliance with Owen. Garvey's visit to the West Coast in 1922 came only a week after the first meeting held by the Friends of Negro Freedom.[30] Thompson's resolve to split his energies between two organizations that held differing points of view on how they were to interact with Garvey ultimately led to the decline of both. Thompson and Owen, however, did realize that what they both had in common with some of the better-off Blacks in the PCNIA was a strong desire to participate in local land speculation. In 1923, the PCNIA became the California Land Development Company, which later formed with other Black organizations to provide loans and investment for Black-owned businesses in the Los Angeles area.[31] As seen in this instance, it was the ideas of Garveyism—Black business development and the pursuit of Black economic self-sufficiency—that outlived these formal organizations and continued to resonate through western racial affairs long after Garvey himself was gone to foreign shores and near obscurity.

On the East Coast, Garvey's movement was in swift decline following the Klan debacle. In the American West, however, the movement's decline was neither as sharp nor as swift as in the East. Months after the Klan meeting, the UNIA chapters that still existed in the major cities along the West Coast continued to remain active even though articles in the *California Eagle* challenged Garvey's positions with headlines such as "Garvey Says: This [Klan] Organization is Alright. What Do You Say?"[32] The movement in the West had in essence progressed far beyond Garvey himself. As it had from the beginning, western Garveyism would take on a form of its own, reflective of the local circumstances that distinguished it from Garveyism's other national and international incarnations. Still central to the character of western Garveyism and its splinter group the PCNIA was a predilection for multiracial and multinational resistance to the forces of white supremacist activism. Charlotta Bass had voiced her observation of this resistance in the *California Eagle* when she was a supporter of the offshoot PCNIA and no longer a loyal Garvey supporter: "Catholics, Jews, Japanese, and Negroes have to be a unit on all political issues in order to fight a certain evil which all of them openly oppose. The whole crowd is opposed by the Ku Klux Klan, so the whole crowd must oppose Ku Klux Klan propaganda."[33]

A part of the reason for this continued impulse towards cooperation was that nationalism among racial groups remained strong in the early twentieth-century west. In the city of San Francisco, UNIA organizer Farr had spread the claim, unlikely as it was, that Garvey and Mahatma Gandhi—leader of the Hindu Revolutionary movement—were once classmates in England, perhaps in an effort to rally Indian nationalists to the UNIA agenda.[34] Black nationalists on the West Coast continued to be inspired by the growing Indian independence movement and Gandhi, even though they did not necessarily agree that nonviolence was a realistic strategy.[35] Fear about this consanguinity among Black and Indian nationalists permeated the American government and caused the US Intelligence Office to warn the Office of Naval Intelligence that "the present Hindu revolutionary movement has definite connections with the Negro agitation in America."[36] In spite of Garvey's disastrous outreach to the KKK, in San Francisco the UNIA remained cohesive throughout the mid-1920s. This continued commitment to interracial cooperation and unification against common oppression may very well have been a primary factor that enabled Garveyism on the West Coast, at least temporarily, to remain a viable movement, despite the eminent decline of Garveyism in the East at the time.

In a larger sense, what transpired in the West reflected the degree to which Garveyism there had matured to much more than the personal cult of a charismatic individual. While classic Garveyism indisputably suffered from the character flaws and misjudgments apparent in Garvey the individual, and as an organization was rendered all but dead by Garvey's arrest, imprisonment, and eventual deportation in the mid-1920s, the ideals that Garvey had trumpeted in his rise to prominence would not disappear from the racial consciousness of the Black population once he had been removed from his position of power. The vision of Black pride and a glorious Black past that Garvey touted in counterpoint to white racist stereotypes aimed at Blacks could not be erased by his deportation. Rather, emerging new scholarship by W.E.B. Du Bois, Carter G. Woodson, J. A. Rogers, and others challenged the transparent pseudoscientific and Eurocentric academic propaganda that had passed for scholarship in the western world to that point. This awakened and subsequently strengthened the idea that Blacks could look to their race, their history, and themselves with pride, and this feeling would never again die out from the struggle for racial justice.

Garvey's emphasis on the need for economic independence as well as his attempts to create Black wealth-generating enterprises had not been ideas uniquely conceived by himself. Earlier Black leaders like Frederick Douglass, Booker T. Washington, and William Monroe Trotter had all to some degree advocated similar objectives. Even Garvey's enemies of his own generation like W.E.B. Du Bois and the NAACP incorporated goals of Black economic power and self-sufficiency in their racial agenda for progress. It was Garvey's grand vision of the BSL and his insistence that once unified, Blacks could rival the economic power of white imperialism in that colonial era, elevated the Black imagination to new heights. Even Garvey's dismal record in failing to bring his ideas to fruition could not destroy the aspirations that vision had inspired in his followers. In the West, Blacks had not just embraced Garvey, they had taken to heart the principles upon which Garveyism was based and were determined to reap the rewards of their implementation even as Garvey himself was forced from the public stage.

The multiracial circumstances of the West allowed such a vision to be seen through a more complex lens that reinforced for Blacks the potential of attacking racism with a more inclusive battle plan. In states like California, Blacks could see that Japanese Americans were advancing economically and they found commonality in the repercussions Japanese suffered due to their success. The 1924 Asian Exclusion Act provided evidence to Blacks of what lengths the government would go to in order to curb the economic success of nonwhites.[37] "The Big Sin committed by the Japanese and that which made them so obnoxious to white California, was their thrift and progress," stated the *Baltimore Afro-American*.[38] Many Blacks felt the government equally feared Black economic success.[39] The sense that all people of color faced a common racial enemy in the West encouraged even Black nationalists to seek partners and build coalitions across racial and cultural lines.

The handwriting announcing the decline of Garvey may have been on the wall by the end of 1922, but Garvey was not the kind of man who would have acknowledged or perhaps even recognized the message, nor meekly acquiesced in its inevitability. Ego, energy, and audacity had been what he used to build his movement, and he sought to save it with application of the same qualities. In November 1923, Garvey returned to California for what would be his last visit to the American West. He toured San Francisco, Oakland, Los Angeles, and San Diego. Because the controversy around Garvey had grown to intense levels by this time, many of the crowds who came out to see Garvey were not UNIA members, but rather curious onlookers.[40] In spite of the PCNIA, the Friends of the Negro, and the general disillusionment of many former Garveyites, Garvey found some success on this trip. As the Los Angeles Black population grew larger, the UNIA continued to admit new members there, and although it was never as strong or as influential as it had once been, the UNIA in Los Angeles stayed intact longer than chapters in other West Coast cities and did not disband until the 1930s.[41] Effective Garvey divisions in other major West Coast urban centers such as Seattle, however, atrophied as Garvey's own personal fortunes declined.

The stories revolving around the influences of Garveyism and its interracial organizing in the rural American West are harder ones to find and tell than the grand speeches and large crowds seen at the height of the movement in the urban centers of the early 1920s. Very often they are stories centered in the smaller rural outposts of Garveyism that took root in such places as Bakersfield, San Bernardino, Pixley, Fresno, and Allensworth, California, and numerous other outlying areas of agricultural work and settlement in western locales from Arizona to the Northwest.

In Carey McWilliams' groundbreaking work *Factories in the Field*, the racial categories of workers are divided into Japanese, Ragheads,[42] Mexicans, and Filipinos.[43] He affected no category for Blacks in spite of the fact that Black workers do appear periodically in his narrative. In Richard Steven Street's massive 870-page tome *Beasts of the Field*, rarely are Black rural laborers included in his analysis of California farmworkers. Yet, there is evidence available to establish both the presence of Black workers in those rural settings and the legacy of Garveyism as well.

During the heyday of Garveyism between 1910 and the early 1920s, an attempt was made to plant the Black colony called "Little Liberia" in Baja California, Mexico (see chapter 2). This was not an isolated attempt at Black colonization in the West. The American West in the early twentieth century saw approximately 200 such Black colonization schemes of various sizes and success.[44] Most were in Oklahoma, a part of what can be called the *near West* for its proximity to the *old South*, where the largest Black population centers were located. Most of the attempts to plant Black towns and settlements in the near West were responses to the dangers and racial violence of Black life in the old South. These had begun as early as the Reconstruction era of the 1870s under the leadership of such men as the famous Pap Singleton in Oklahoma.[45] As more Blacks moved further west in later years, they too sought safety and economic independence in all-Black settlements in rural areas. In California, for example, the San Joaquin Valley became the site of numerous Black settlements over the years, especially after California turned to cotton agriculture in the early twentieth century and eventually became the second largest cotton-producing state in the union after Texas. Black workers were imported into the cotton fields of the state because of their long history of experience with that crop. These workers were less protected and more exploited on average than Blacks who created semi-independent Black towns and settlements in the state.

California cotton workers had an especially difficult time in the fields. The heat was often well over 100 degrees, living conditions were squalid, and work hours were long. Although cotton had been grown in California since the early nineteenth century when Spanish missionaries cultivated it to clothe Indigenous Americans, it became even more desirable when the boll weevil destroyed crops in the American South (the boll weevil could not survive the arid climate of central California) and the outbreak of World War I raised demand for cotton.[46] By 1929, more than 30 percent of the country's cotton farms were in California.[47] And where there was cotton in California, Black population centers were to be found.

In California, twelve all-Black communities including incorporated towns and unofficial settlements existed in this era altogether, many located in the cotton-growing district of the Central Valley like the ones listed above.[48] Near rural Pixley, California, in the Central Valley, were the Black settlements of Teviston and Alkali. The all-Black settlement of Centerville was seventeen miles east of Fresno while the similar Black settlement of Raisin City was seventeen miles to the west of Fresno. Fowler was another all-Black rural settlement eleven miles south of Fresno. The all-Black community of Mayflower and adjacent tract Sunset were located near Bakersfield and have now been absorbed into that city. These settlements boasted few urban amenities, but they did provide a measure of collective identity, safety, and mutual support among the Blacks who lived there. Some Blacks also operated independent freehold farms in various parts of the West. UNIA divisions existed in several of the settlements as well. In 1920s Fresno, there was an active Garvey division that would have both influenced and in turn reflected the aspirations of the Black settlements around it, such as Raisin City and Fowler.

One particular all-Black town of some notoriety was the unincorporated town of Allensworth, which is located in Tulare County, California, halfway between Bakersfield and Fresno. In its heyday,

Allensworth represented a model for all-Black independent towns. As a result, scholars and locals have given it so much attention that they have created a public record that can be mined for insights. The town's founder Allen Allensworth had a remarkable life and career. He was born into slavery in Louisville, Kentucky, but escaped during the Civil War to fight for the Union as a seaman in the Union Navy. In 1880 and 1884, he served as the only Black delegate from Kentucky at the Republican National Convention and acquired an appointment as a captain in the all-Black 24th Regiment, one of the famed Buffalo Soldiers' units. He held this position for twenty years before retiring in 1906 as a lieutenant colonel, the highest rank of any Black officer in the Army during the time period.[49] The combination of his strong Christian faith and his roots in American slavery probably contributed to his support of Booker T. Washington's model of industry and lifting oneself up by the bootstraps mentality. This was well in line with the tenets of Garveyism, as Marcus Garvey himself was an avid admirer of Booker T. Washington.[50]

Allensworth worked the lecture circuits in California, where he spoke on Washington's points of racial uplift and economic self-determination. Along the way, he met a teacher named William Payne, who shared his vision of Black economic independence as the primary mode of social uplift for the race. Together, along with other members including Dr. W. H. Peck, J. W. Palmer, a Nevada miner, and Harry P. Mitchell,[51] they founded the California Colony and Home Promoting Association in 1908 and worked to find an acceptable location to establish their town. According to historian Lawrence de Graaf, with only ten dollars to their name, the "Association entered into a promotion agreement with three white-owned real estate companies that owned large blocks of land in the San Joaquin Valley. The three companies platted an eighty-acre townsite. . . . Evidence suggests that the black consortium contracted with the companies for some unrecorded amount of money to secure African-American settlers for the townsite and got the companies' agreement to reserve the surrounding lands for Black farmers."[52] Within three years, the association sold "more than four hundred parcels of land valued at $112, 000."[53] The town founded a school (which doubled as a center for political rallies), a library, and a post office. Payne, who became a teacher in the town he helped found, stated, "One of the outstanding things I remember about Allensworth was the library. It was the best equipped small library that I have ever seen, and I spent many happy hours in there, reading and taking books out. And all of us read a great deal. There were no illiterate children in that area."[54]

Allensworth himself met an untimely fate when he was killed by two white motorcyclists while walking in Monrovia, California, in 1914.[55] The town that he helped to establish, however, continued, albeit increasingly on shaky ground. The white-owned Pacific Farming Company, which had initially provided land for the town, eventually sought to take away the town's water rights. To hasten the town's demise, the Santa Fe Railroad was diverted to another nearby town, effectively denying much-needed transportation and commercial opportunities for Allensworth. Yet, it continued to progress in some ways. In 1921, an NAACP chapter was created. About that time a formal UNIA division was also organized. Reportedly "some residents supported the nationalist politics of Marcus Garvey. The opinion leaders were well-known and referred to collectively as the town philosophers."[56] The small size in population of Allensworth and close ties amongst townspeople suggest the likelihood that, as in Los Angeles, these two organizations worked more in harmony than was characteristic of their East Coast counterparts at this time. As made clear through townspeople's recollections of living in Allensworth, on the individual level at least, members of the NAACP and the UNIA coexisted as neighbors in the town and not as enemies.

Like many Black attempts at economic independence in the racial climate of the early twentieth century, the town of Allensworth did not survive. Low water supplies and the loss of the train stop forced Black residents to relocate as the 1920s wound down. By the late 1920s many Black farmers had lost their land, and work on the white farms became the only option for employment in the rural areas. "Cotton had come into the San Joaquin Valley and Allensworth became a place people lived during the cotton season, and then moved on."[57] Even though the town was only temporary, there was clearly a sense of Black nationalism and Black pride in the community rooted in the tenets of Booker T. Washington and Marcus Garvey. However, there was more to the story.

Interestingly, although Allensworth was settled by Black people, it was not an all-Black town in the strictest sense of the word. In the oral history of a woman who grew up as a child in Allensworth, Alice Royal recalls her second grade classroom: "I remember the big dictionary and the potbellied stove, playing hopscotch and jump rope with the other girls. There was one white child and a few Mexicans."[58] Furthermore, town member Josephine Hackett "recalls how her mother sold milk to the Mexican section hands."[59] Because the town had only a Baptist church, townspeople held Methodist services in the school and Seventh Day Adventists met in homes, while the Latino residents "held their services in Catholic churches of neighboring communities."[60] Clearly, from this history of what has always been considered an all-Black town, there were residents who were not Black, making Allensworth an interracial cooperative.

On the other side of the racial playing field, the white landowners and big agricultural concerns of the day had one primary driving force in their behavior: they needed labor, and lots of it. Farmers were convinced that Blacks and Mexicans were the ideal racial groups for cotton picking. As the harvesting season approached they ran advertisements in the daily newspapers throughout the South and Southwestern states imploring people to come to work. One such ad read, "Wanted-1000 cotton pickers for the Imperial Valley,

California. Wages, $1.00 per 100 pounds. Picking begins September 1. Colonists rates will be in effect on all railroads. Joseph R. Loftus Company, the California Cotton People, El Centro, California."[61] Other workers who came to work in the cotton fields were deemed too lazy. Of the American Indigenous the *Imperial Valley Press* wrote, "Their scheme is to get enough cotton in a sack to make a comfortable cushion, and then sit down on the sack and the bolls within reach, holding a branch with one hand and carefully extracting the lint with the other."[62]

East Asian Indians were deemed equally ill-suited to the job. However, Mexicans and Blacks were considered ideal. Like Blacks, Mexicans coming to labor in the fields began to congregate, forming all-Mexican colonies in California. Whites often reacted negatively towards both all-Black and all-Mexican towns. Reporting on the town of "Little Mexico" near El Centro, the *Imperial Daily Standard* complained that "cotton picking time is attracting a doubtful looking bunch of all shades and kinds."[63] Nevertheless, white farmers seeking cheap labor to supply their growing businesses across California trucked Blacks in from the southern states, and Mexicans poured in to escape the Mexican revolution and its aftermath.

Regardless of which group was determined to be better suited for cotton picking, the need for labor overruled all other factors. As a result, other workers were recruited as well. By 1910 "growers advertised for pickers across the Southwest, luring blacks, Koreans, South Asians, Japanese, Filipinos, Puerto Ricans, Mexicans, and [American] Indians from Arizona."[64] Although Blacks made up a very small percentage of the agricultural labor force compared to Mexicans, their presence should still be considered. Cotton was not the only agricultural product that boomed in California. The citrus crops also had high demands for labor as well as crops of grapes, lettuce, and tomatoes. All of these crops were dependent on seasonal migrant labor, and that labor force evolved to be both poor and populations of color represented by numerous nationalities.

Thus, even after the decline of the classic Garvey era, the conditions of close physical proximity of diverse nonwhite populations struggling against harsh life circumstances and hostile racial antagonists within a shared white supremacist–dominated environment mirrored the conditions in urban areas. These had coalesced in the earlier period of Garveyism to inspire multicultural coalitions in these rural working populations of the West as well. Under such circumstances, it is reasonable to conclude that even after the decline of the classic organizational high point of Garveyism in the West, the philosophies of Garveyism as practiced in the West continued to influence interracial dynamics in a less formal but nonetheless important way in the rural outposts. Indeed, support of this ongoing influence can be found sprinkled within the generally sparse record of life in these Black outposts.

However, the 1920s multiracial Garveyism that had been so influential in the West would not be the ideological vehicle through which the multiracial and multinational vision of unified opposition to white racial oppression would move forward into the challenging years of the Great Depression. During the increasingly class conscious 1930s, the appeal of Garveyism, like that of other nationalist movements, was doomed to wane. This was due in large part to the fundamental fact that the objective of Garveyism's economic program was not to destroy capitalism or offer an alternative to it, but to embrace it in the Black and colored worlds. As such, in the 1930s it would eventually lose out to a more aggressive and expansive challenge to capitalism in the contest for the allegiance of exploited populations of color. In short, Garveyism would be eclipsed by the appeals of Bolshevism—communism—as the ideological weapon of choice for many seeking relief from the woes of economic depression, spawned by global capitalism.

Indeed, the communists positioned themselves in many ways as heirs apparent to the kind of global anti-imperialism that had been the hallmark of Garvey rhetoric in the heyday of his popularity.

Global communism even built initial credibility in the international anti-imperialist community by assisting some of the same nationalist groups, such as the Ghadarites, that West Coast Garveyism had allied with in the early 1920s.[65]

The shift from nationalism to communism in the mid-1920s through the 1930s was not unique to the Black community. The Ghadar Party, which held many parallels to Garveyism, also flirted with communism in this era. The first president of the Ghadar Party, Sohan Singh Bhakna, who had organized the Party along the West Coast after white racists attacked Indians in Washington and Vancouver, Canada, also turned to communism. Bhakna was convicted of attempting to overthrow the English colonial government in the Lahore Conspiracy Trials in 1915. During the trial, "special emphasis was put on the Pacific Coast as the center of a global Indian revolutionary movement."[66] Some anti-colonial leaders were executed, and Bhakna was convicted and jailed for sixteen years. The Communist Party was partly responsible for his release in 1928: the British government had initially sought to extend his imprisonment, inducing Bhakna to go on a hunger strike. The communists used his resulting illness to pressure his release.[67] Such support for early anti-colonial Indian nationalism built goodwill for the communists in international racial developments in the post-Garvey years.

Clearly, some Indian nationalists, like many Black nationalists, turned to communism as a possible route to escape white racism and as a way to find economic opportunity. Indian nationalists and Black nationalists were in communication with each other during the height of the Garvey era, and it would be reasonable to assume that these two nationalist groups, both flirting with communism as a way out of the racially and economically oppressive climate they both found themselves in, continued to organize against their common foe.

Initially, communists were little concerned with race, but, according to Robin Kelley, by the mid-1920s "popular support for black nationalist movements within the African-American working-class communities, compelled the CPUSA [Communist Party of the USA] to seriously reconsider its approach to the 'Negro Question.'"[68] Garvey's view of communism was divided. He saw a distinct difference between communism in the United States and communism in Russia, especially under Lenin. In an editorial published in the *Negro World*, Garvey wrote, "Not one but the four hundred millions of us should mourn over the death of this great man, because Russia promised great hope not only to Negroes but to the weaker peoples of the world."[69] Yet, like many Black communists by the 1930s, Garvey was disillusioned by American communists who were believed to hold "white chauvinism within their ranks." For example, in 1922, well-known author and poet, "Claude McKay, had charged white American communists with racism at the fourth Comintern congress."[70]

As it turned out, many white American communists of the early 1930s would prove to be false prophets in the anti-racism struggle. The Party proclaimed itself the champion of rights for Black Americans. However, there is much evidence to suggest that the CPUSA was more committed to serving the interest of Russian foreign policy than an all-out fight for anti-racism and anti-imperialist principles in the 1930s. Without a doubt, there were some individual communists who took the rhetoric of racial equality seriously and tried to incorporate that principle into their individual behavior. However, attitudes would not change based simply on rhetoric. Many influential Black leaders left the Communist Party once it became apparent that the promise of equality did not necessarily translate into action. An example of Party members' frustrations with racism within the Party can be seen in the experiences of George Padmore, the West Indian journalist and author. The Party was unsupportive of his organizing work and uninterested in his concerns over the dangers that Black workers faced within the Party. By the mid-1930s, Padmore had severed ties with the Communist

Party due to the "processes of his frustration with the racism he witnessed within the Party, which stifled his initiative and relegated him to a 'child-like' status within the movement."[71]

During the decade of the 1930s, bitter conflicts between the CPUSA and the older traditional racial protest organizations eventually erupted for control of the anti-racism agenda. Most notable was the no-holds-barred battle between the CPUSA and the NAACP for primacy in the defense of the Scottsboro Boys, a group of nine young Black men in Alabama. In the 1930s, the Scottsboro Boys had been judicially railroaded into long prison terms after being falsely accused of the gang rape of two white women. Serious questions about the alleged circumstances of the encounter did not deter the courts from dispensing automatic death sentences to eight of the nine defendants. Both the NAACP and the Communist Party wanted control over the case, which made national headlines. The CPUSA ultimately claimed victory in that battle over the NAACP to lead the defense, although they were not able to completely exonerate the Black men or vacate the long prison sentences they received. They were, however, able to prevent any from being executed. This combat with the CPUSA had been so bitter that well into the 1950s the NAACP refused to allow Communist Party members to join the NAACP.[72] These decisions had a major impact on Black leadership.

In California, the inaction of the local NAACP branches to speak out for the Scottsboro Boys case spurred some frustrated Black Californians to turn towards the Communist Party. In Los Angeles, Loren Miller, a lawyer, activist, and writer for the *California Eagle* in the 1930s, was greatly impacted by the Scottsboro case. As a result of local NAACP inaction, Miller, along with a number of other Black activists in the Los Angeles area, gravitated towards the Communist Party.[73] Another Black leader, Pettis Perry, a communist organizer for the Cannery and Agricultural Workers Industrial Union in California, was also greatly interested in the Scottsboro Boys case. According to historian Josh Sides, his frustrations over

119

the local NAACP and their refusal to openly stand up for the Scottsboro boys led him "to give every free hour to spreading the news of the Scottsboro case to as many people as [he] possibly could."[74]

However, an international event called into question for many Blacks the commitment of the Party to true interracial anti-imperialism. In 1935, Italy invaded Ethiopia. In an article published in *The Crisis*, George Padmore alleged that "the Soviet Union had initially refused to support Ethiopia at the League of Nations."[75] In his article titled "Ethiopia and World Politics," Padmore argued that Lenin and Trotsky, the early leaders of the Russian revolution, had once divided the world into imperialist and anti-imperialist nations, but "since the defeat of the revolutionary movement in Germany and Central Europe resulting in the rise of Hitlerism on the one hand, and the threat of war in the East on the other hand, the present Soviet leaders have changed their foreign policy, as they no longer have any faith in the ability of the workers of Europe and American to defend Russia if attacked."[76] However, though his views were no doubt shared by many within the Black diaspora, Padmore's assertions that Russia was silent regarding the Italian invasion were in fact not accurate. The Soviet Foreign Minister, Maxim Litvinov, was the first within the League of Nations to criticize Italy for its invasion of Ethiopia.[77]

For many American Black nationalists and even Black mainstream integrationists, Ethiopia held a treasured idealized place in Black identity politics as the last truly free Black nation in Africa. The invasion of Ethiopia strengthened the Pan-African movement, worked to create a united front amongst Black organizations throughout the world, and reinvigorated the Black nationalist movement. As these events unfolded both nationally and in the American West, the UNIA's former multiracial organizing lost significant power in matters of racial progress. The viciousness of the current inter-radical battles stood in stark contrast to the potential reality of true multiracial unity that had been possible in the 1920s when the UNIA had been a major player in the West in such matters.

The other major development that contributed to the disappearance of the kind of coalition building that held great potential when Garveyism held sway in the West was the transformation of an old anti-imperialist ally of the UNIA into a new pro-imperialist enemy. Specifically, Japan had transformed itself from the anti-imperial champion of the post–World War I Paris peace talks into a growing imperial aggressor in Asia and the Pacific Basin.[78] In terms of the kind of alliances that western Garveyism had tried with some success to build in the early 1920s, it mattered not what complicated motives drove this Japanese transformation. Regarding India, China, Southeast Asia, Korea, and the Pacific Islands, the brutal Japanese imperialism of the 1930s subverted any possibility of nationalist groups from those areas ever working again with Japan against white American racist oppression within the American West. Organizationally, the vision of a grand global unity amongst people of color against the forces of racism that had seemed at least possible in the western version of Garveyism in the 1920s was now a dead letter in the post-Garvey politics of the 1930s.

By the time Marcus Garvey died in London in 1940, and with the advent of World War II in the 1940s, the conflicts over race and imperialism would consume the entire planet in a cataclysm of bloodshed and violence that pushed the human species to the verge of self-extinction with the coming of the military atomic age. The postwar success of anti-colonial movements in Africa, Southeast Asia, the Asian subcontinent, and the Middle East would only be marginally less transformative than the war itself had been. Indeed, the ramifications of these events still haunt the world into the twenty-first century. It is, of course, tantalizing under those circumstances to wonder what might have been achieved had the great potential for multiracial, multinational cooperation that flared brightly but briefly in the western American Garvey movement in the early 1920s been realized—a better world, perhaps, or just a different one?

CONCLUSION

The goal of this work is to provide a new understanding of Black nationalism in the early twentieth century through a global lens and within the broader context of a period in which people of color from around the world experienced similar oppressive circumstances. Although differing nationalist groups had distinct needs and requirements, there were times when these groups came together to work towards a common goal. An analysis of Garveyism on the West Coast is the perfect place from which to make these global connections. However, without a foundation in the global events of World War I and its effect on the Black diaspora, it would be difficult to understand how the conditions of the American West were uniquely conducive to the interracial organizing of seemingly racially exclusive organizations like the Garvey movement.

Throughout the twentieth century, Garveyism represented an important ideological and political movement that had far-reaching effects among people of color. Black nationalism was one element in the rise of nationalisms around the world. As Black populations—regardless of national origin—descended on European battlefields and camps where they were assigned to hard labor and received substandard treatment in comparison to their white counterparts, the realization of an international shared experience among Black people became apparent. Just as Blacks experienced similar conditions through their service in their respective countries, they also shared the same frustrations of coming home to the same racially oppressive circumstances they had left behind. For people of color, the collective frustration of risking their lives to protect white freedom while remaining in poverty and enduring continued discrimination became an overwhelming force upon the return of the Black soldiers after the war. As a result, race riots broke out across the globe. Black veterans, now trained in combat and armed, were no longer willing to suffer the unjust conditions to which they had previously been subjected.

It was this reality that propelled Garvey's message of Black pride, economic Black independence, and militant self-defense to the forefront of Black life in the Western Hemisphere. The military trappings of the movement, which included soldier uniforms for the African Legion, a flag, an anthem, a Black Star nurse division, and parades and marches, resonated with former war veterans and instilled racial pride. Furthermore, Black women, who could otherwise not serve in a white army, found in the Black Cross nurses in the Garvey movement a purpose and position in which they felt important.

In reaction to Garvey's message of retaliation against the status quo and his declaration to take up arms in self-defense, colonial governments throughout South America, the Caribbean, and Africa banned the *Negro World*, the official publication of Garvey's movement, in their attempts to squash the movement and because they believed Marcus Garvey's message to be a call for Black violence. However, rather than diminishing the movement, the ban of the newspaper actually made Garveyism more popular and caused sales and distribution of the *Negro World* to soar.

This expansion of Garveyism in the context of the World War I era represents an important component to understanding Garveyism in the American West. As soldiers returned to their homes in the Southern United States, it became apparent to many that they could no longer tolerate the Jim Crow racism and lynching that they had experienced before the war. Many of these former soldiers moved north, but some also went west. The small numbers of Blacks in the West represented one significant factor as to why transnational organizing became such a crucial component of the Garvey movement in this region. Furthermore, nonwhite groups such as those from India, who had suffered under colonialism and fought in World War I for their English colonial oppressor, shared a common experience with Blacks in the West. Not only had they fought in the same war, but they lived in a country that discriminated against them in the most violent and humiliating ways. Like Blacks in the Caribbean and the United States, Indians gained little from their efforts in the war, as the British continued to subjugate and oppress Indian citizens. Those Indians who immigrated to the West Coast of the US seeking a better life for themselves were often met with suspicion there. The feelings of a common shared experience between Black Americans and Indians greatly concerned both the British and US officials, who put them under constant surveillance.[1]

The West Coast, however, provided a space that was conducive to interracial and international organizing. Angel Island, the immigrant entryway to the West that operated from 1910 to 1940, brought a million immigrants[2] through its doors, including Chinese, Japanese, Indians, Filipinos, Mexicans, and others. As immigrants of color entered the country through Angel Island, white supremacists on the West Coast, perceiving an "Asian invasion," mobilized in an effort to intimidate these groups. Nonwhite immigrants and citizens, who all were subject to the discrimination of racist organizations like the Asiatic Exclusion League and the Ku Klux Klan, found themselves in an environment favorable to interracial organizing, even as these same groups competed among themselves for the small number of jobs that workers of color could get.

Yet, while job competition remained aggressive at times, larger global issues often took center stage among nationalist groups. One example can be seen in the interactions of Blacks and Japanese. In the post–World War I negotiations at the Paris Peace Conference, the fact that the Japanese government attempted to add an amendment to the Treaty of Versailles was a very important component in the desire of Garveyites in the West to align with Japanese and Japanese Americans. The irony that the Japanese were as dangerous a colonizer in the Pacific as the Europeans were globally did not seem to trouble most Black nationalists in the West. Perhaps the discrimination that Japanese Americans suffered in the West alongside Blacks overrode what the Japanese government was capable of across the ocean. Similar to the discrimination suffered by Japanese Americans, Chinese and Chinese Americans also were victims of white supremacy. According to historian Marc Gallicchio, "African Americans were not wholly indifferent to China, rather they assumed that racial affinity would eventually overcome artificial Japanese and Chinese differences."[3] Garvey, who had hoped to strike a financial deal with Japanese banks to fund his Black Star Line, worked to convince Blacks that the Japanese relationship with China was to be blamed on the whites, declaring "[The white capitalists] have subsidized the Chinese to reject every proposal of Japan, to cause them to believe that the Japanese hate them and want only to take away their country. The Japanese realize that a certain propaganda has been at work against them in the East, and they are going to meet propaganda with propaganda."[4]

Although the war certainly represented the catalyst for the rapid expansion of Garveyism across the world, it was the Black Star Line that sustained the movement once it had spread. The global shipping trade is probably one of the most important, yet one of the most understudied by historians, modes of colonial wealth. Colonially dominated spaces like India, Africa, and the Caribbean experienced economic subjugation very much through their lack of control of maritime trade. The inability to participate in trade in India became the very business around which nationalism formed. Similarly, the lack of control of global trade among West Africans and the Black populations of the Caribbean basin drew thousands to the Garvey movement and its promise of an all-Black shipping line. On the West Coast, the notion of the BSL arrived before the establishment of most of the UNIA divisions there, especially those in port cities, and it is not unreasonable to suggest that this interest in the BSL contributed to the desire of West Coast Blacks to establish such an organization. By 1921 UNIA chapters, thanks in great measure to the BSL opening, had increased from 95 to 418 across the country, with more applications awaiting processing.[5] By 1925 there were upwards of twenty-five chapters in the West.

Though the Garvey movement sharply declined with his arrest and deportation, Garvey and the BSL left a lasting impression, especially in West Africa. In 1957, Ghana's first president, Kwame Nkrumah, was heavily inspired by Garvey's movement. As a result, Ghanaians named a series of businesses after the BSL, including the Black Star Line Shipping Corporation, created in the 1960s, and in the 1990s, the Black Star Line Cooperative Credit Union.[6] The BSL inspired others as well. In Oakland, California, there is a Black Star Line All-Star swim team. Out of Chicago, there was a play about the Black Star Line and in Ohio, a Black Star Line Entertainment Company. Though Garvey's BSL was not economically a success for the UNIA and its shareholders, it is clear that its psychological impact on Blacks worldwide helped to inspire large numbers of followers and propelled the movement to levels it would never have seen had the BSL not existed. Though the notion of a "Back to Africa" movement is one that is most often remembered by historians and Afrocentric scholars in association with Garvey, it was the Black Star Line that actually created the explosive and exciting possibilities for Black economic equality in the early twentieth century.

Although many Garvey scholars place full blame for the BSL's failure on Garvey's mismanagement, factors beyond Garvey's control contributed to the collapse of that enterprise. Indeed, as historian David Cronon observed, "although Garvey managed to collect a surprisingly large sum of money for the line, the purchase of ships at grossly inflated prices and the attempt to enter an industry plagued by ruinous competition would have spelled out disaster for even a more soundly managed corporation."[7] However, where the shipping line did succeed was in its ability to inspire the vision of Black economic independence and the possibility of a global enterprise that would incorporate the colored world and facilitate the attack on white economic oppression.

Ultimately, disillusionment with the BSL and the reality that the line was not a viable commercial enterprise contributed to the decline of Garveyism in the West. Upon discovery that the line was not viable, the largest UNIA division in Los Angeles splintered as two-thirds of the organization left to form the Pacific Coast Negro Association (PCNA). This faction still aligned itself with the tenets of Garveyism but refused to further contribute financially to the UNIA. Furthermore, Garvey's attempts to align the UNIA with the Ku Klux Klan sparked nationwide outrage against Garvey and marked the swift decline of the movement throughout the United States.

As interesting as the possibilities of multiracial Garveyism in the urban centers proved to be in the Far West, Garveyism in the rural areas may also have worked across racial lines. Little is known about Garveyism in these small towns; however, there were a number of UNIA divisions spread throughout the agricultural west, especially in California. Just as they had in the cities, Blacks made up a very small minority amongst larger working-class populations of color. It is unreasonable to assume that Garveyites in the rural areas worked as a Black-only movement. Even as the evidence is circumstantial, the likelihood of interracial organizing in small rural towns is strong. Towns like Fresno, which had a UNIA division, as well as Tulare and Hanford, which both had all-Black neighborhoods at their peripheries, also had a multiracial merchant class, most of whom were Jewish, Portuguese, Japanese, and Mexican.[8] In all probability, there was also a Black business owner or two in these areas.

According to historian Devra Weber, when strikes occurred the merchants "undercut the grower's efforts to starve workers into submission"[9] by donating food, shelter, and meeting spaces to the strikers, even upon threat of bodily injury from the farm owners. Through these moments of interracial solidarity, it can be determined that, just as in the urban centers, where nationalists worked across racial boundaries, the same occurred in the rural areas. Nationalism formed around labor, and Black nationalists themselves congregated in small towns like Allensworth, Fresno, Bakersfield, and others. It is also conceivable that although there were times when white farm owners successfully created racial division, there were clearly times when conditions were bad enough to compel racial unity.

As the 1920s came to a close, Garveyism appeared to have faded out in the rural areas just as it did in most of the urban centers. The primary reason for this is of course the deportation of Marcus Garvey himself, which disbanded the headquarters in Harlem and weakened the strength of the movement globally. However, other factors may also have led to Garveyism's demise in the West. Small Black towns and neighborhoods did not survive the Great Depression because many Blacks, such as those who lived in Allensworth, California, eventually migrated to the larger cities in search of work. The Black nationalist message of Black pride, economic uplift, and the recognition of a glorious Black past would live on, but some Blacks gravitated towards the Communist Party, as did some Mexicans, Anglos, and Jews.[10]

Garveyism was a capitalist movement which, with the failure of the shipping line and economic progress, allowed the CPUSA to draw disillusioned Blacks into its organization. (Internal fighting also helped to break up the Garvey movement. But it should be noted that these general trends did not represent the entire Black population, and many held fast to the tenets of Garveyism.) The attention Japanese nationalists gave to Black American grievances served them well as they maintained some Black support, even those associated with the CPUSA. The CPUSA itself, however, lost considerable Black membership to Pan Africanism and other organizations because some members perceived the Communist Party as tainted by its own internal racism.

This turn to communism by nationalist groups in the West seems to be a logical progression given the way that the Great Depression affected communities of color more significantly than it affected others. The inability to maintain economic independence, coupled with the daily realities of racial discrimination, labor exploitation, and a lack of access to a strong political voice, pushed Blacks, Japanese, Indians, Mexicans, and other racial minorities towards the communist program. The possibility of economic independence from the Anglo world and the promise of racial inclusiveness, as well as communism's anti-capitalist stance and its locations on the margins of the larger white American society, made communism initially appealing to people of color.

Just as we saw with Garveyism, the Ghadar Party, and the Mexican and Japanese nationalists in the American West, the fact that these groups were yet again moving in the same direction during the same time period brings into question the extent to which they may have worked together towards these common ends. As seen in the experiences of other groups of color and their connections with Black nationalism, the patterns of interracial organizing continued even beyond the Garvey movement. Through interracial organizing against a common white oppressor, groups of color in the West, regardless of size or economic persuasion, became more powerful when they worked together.

NOTES

INTRODUCTION

1. Some excellent books on Garvey include: E. David Cronon, *Black Moses: The Story of Marcus Garvey and the Universal Negro Improvement Association* (Madison: University of Wisconsin Press, 1955 and 1969); Tony Martin, *Race First: The Ideological and Organizational Struggles of Marcus Garvey and the Universal Negro Improvement Association* (Dover, MA: The Majority Press, 1976); John Henrik Clarke, *Marcus Garvey and the Vision of Africa* (New York: Vintage Books, 1974); Judith Stein, *The World of Marcus Garvey: Race and Class in Modern Society* (Baton Rouge: Louisiana State University Press, 1986); Ula Taylor, *The Veiled Garvey: Life and Times of Amy Jacques Garvey* (Chapel Hill: University of North Carolina Press, 2002); Colin Grant, *Negro with a Hat: The Rise and Fall of Marcus Garvey* (New York: Oxford University Press, 2008); Mary G. Rolinson, *Grassroots Garveyism: The Universal Negro Improvement Association in the Rural South 1920–1927* (Chapel Hill: University of North Carolina Press, 2007).
2. A deeper discussion of the financial crisis Garvey found himself in during the early years of the UNIA in Jamaica can be found in Grant, *Negro with a Hat*, 66.
3. Amy Jacques Garvey, ed., *Philosophy and Opinions of Marcus Garvey* (Dover, MA: The Majority Press, 1986[1923 and 1925]), 212.

4. You can access these recordings through the UCLA African Studies Center online at https://www.international.ucla.edu/asc/mgpp/audio

5. I capitalize the word Black because it is used to replace the outdated term Negro. Black nationalists and Black leaders, such as Hubert Harrison and W.E.B. DuBois, fought hard at one time to convince whites to capitalize the word Negro in white newspapers and printed works. In respect of this effort, I choose to capitalize the word Black whenever referring to a people of Africa or African descent. Since whites do not share a similar historical struggle in terms of racial respect in American culture, I do not capitalize white.

6. See Michael Newton, *White Robes and Burning Crosses: A History of the Ku Klux Klan from 1866* (Jefferson, NC: McFarland and Company, Inc., 2014).

7. See Rolinson, *Grassroots Garveyism*.

8. Gilbert Osofsky, *Harlem: The Making of a Ghetto* (New York: Harper Torchbooks, 1963), 128.

9. Cronon, *Black Moses*, 220–21.

10. Theodore G. Vincent, *Black Power and the Garvey Movement* (Berkeley, CA: The Ramparts Press, 1970), 9.

11. Ibid., 207.

12. Rolinson, *Grassroots Garveyism*, 134.

13. Some of these include: Frederick Douglass Opie, "Garveyism and Labor Organization on the Caribbean Coast of Guatemala, 1920–1921," *The Journal of African American History* 94, no. 2 (Spring 2009): 153–71; Robin Dearmon Jenkins, "Linking up the Golden Gate: Garveyism in the San Francisco Bay Area, 1919–1925," *Journal of Black Studies* 39, no. 2 (November 2008): 266–80; Michael O. West, "The Seeds Are Sown: The Impact of Garveyism in Zimbabwe in the Interwar Years," *The International Journal of African Historical Studies* 35, no. 2/3 (2002): 335–62; John Henrik Clarke,

"Marcus Garvey: The Harlem Years," *The Black Scholar* 5, no. 4, *Black History* (December 1973–1974), 17–23; Mark Christian, ed., "Special Issue: Marcus Garvey and the Universal Negro Improvement Association: New Perspectives on Philosophy, Religion, Micro-Studies, Unity, and Practice," *Journal of Black Studies* 39, no. 2, (November 2008): 163–65; Ronald Harpelle, "Cross Currents in the Western Caribbean: Marcus Garvey and the UNIA in Central America," *Caribbean Studies* 31, no. 1 (January–June 2003): 35–73; W. F. Elkins, "Marcus Garvey, the "Negro World," and the British West Indies: 1919–1920," *Science and Society* 36, no. 1 (Spring 1972): 63–77.

14. See W.E.B. Du Bois, *The World and Africa: An Inquiry into the Part which Africa has Played in World History* (New York: International Publishers, 1965).

15. Throughout this work, I will use the term Indian to describe those residents of Southeast Asian descent (from India). I will use the term Indigenous to refer to the indigenous peoples from the North American continent. Their origins span the thousands of years before colonial settlements became permanent fixtures on the continent. On the African continent as well as in the Americas, the term Native brings with it negative, racist connotations which I do not wish to replicate in my own work, so I choose not to use it.

CHAPTER I

1. See C. Vann Woodward, *Origins of the New South 1877–1913* (Baton Rouge: Louisiana State University Press 1971); Leon Litwack, *Trouble in Mind: Black Southerners in the Age of Jim Crow* (New York: Vintage Publishers, 1999); Nell Irvin Painter, *Exodusters: Black Migration to Kansas after Reconstruction* (New York: W.W. Norton & Company, 1986); Douglas A. Blackmon, *Slavery by Another Name: The Re-enslavement of Black Americans from the Civil War to World War I* (New

York: Doubleday Publishing, 2008).

2. W.E.B. Du Bois, "The Lynching Industry 1919," *The Crisis* 19, no. 4 (February 1920): 185.

3. "Riot A National Disgrace," *The St. Louis Argus* VI, no. 12 (July 6, 1917), 1.

4. For more reading on this subject see: Louis A. Pérez Jr., *Cuba and the United States: Ties of Singular Intimacy*; Jason M. Colby, *The Business of Empire: United Fruit, Race, and the U.S. Expansion in Central America* (Ithaca, NY: Cornell University Press, 2011); Tanya Katerí Hernández, *Racial Subordination in Latin America: The Role of the State, Customary Law, and the New Civil Rights Response* (New York: Cambridge University Press, 2013).

5. B. W. Higman, *A Concise History of the Caribbean* (New York: Cambridge University Press, 2011), 209.

6. Ibid., 227–30.

7. Avi Chomsky, "Afro-Jamaican Traditions and Labor Organizing on United Fruit Company Plantations in Costa Rica, 1910," *Journal of Social History* 28, no. 4 (Summer 1995): 837.

8. Colby, *The Business of Empire*, 94.

9. Ibid., 92.

10. Ibid., 114.

11. Ibid., 99.

12. Julian White and Jurg Meier, *Handbook of Clinical Toxicology of Animal Venoms and Poisons*, CRC Press (August 1995), 312; also in *Tico Times*, Costa Rica's online daily newspaper owned by Producciones Magnolia: ticotimes.net.

13. See Colby, *The Business of Empire*, 104.

14. Ron Harpelle, "Cross Currents in the Western Caribbean: Marcus Garvey and the UNIA in Central America," in "Garveyism and the Universal Negro Improvement Association in the Hispanic Caribbean," special issue of *Caribbean Studies*

31, no. 1 (January–June 2003): 48.

15. Ibid.

16. In 1914, Garvey returned to his home in Jamaica, where he started his first UNIA organization. When he first arrived in the United States, he came with the intention to raise money in order to create a school in Jamaica that would emulate Booker T. Washington's Tuskegee Institute in Alabama.

17. Robert Hill, ed., "World War I" by Richard Smith, *UNIA Papers* (Durham, NC: Duke University Press, 2011), XI: cclxxv.

18. Robert B. Edgerton, *Hidden Heroism: Black Soldiers in America's Wars* (Boulder, CO: Westview Press, 2002), 71.

19. Thomas A. Britten, *American Indians in World War I: At Home and at War* (Albuquerque: University of New Mexico Press, 1997), 57.

20. Ibid., 84.

21. Ibid., 123.

22. Ibid., 57.

23. Chad L. Williams, *Torchbearers of Democracy: African American Soldiers in World War I Era* (Chapel Hill: University of North Carolina Press, 2010), 56.

24. Chandler Owen, "The Failure of the Negro Leaders," *The Messenger* (January 1918): 23.

25. W.E.B. Du Bois, "Close Ranks," *The Crisis* 16, no. 3 (July 1918): 111.

26. Edgerton, *Hidden Heroism*, 90.

27. Ibid., 82–83.

28. Ibid., 101.

29. Quoted in Williams, *Torchbearers of Democracy*, 109–10.

30. Ibid., 111.

31. Edgerton, *Hidden Heroism*, 99.

32. Du Bois, "Close Ranks," 111.

33. Jeffrey Perry, *Hubert Harrison: The Voice of Harlem Radicalism*, 1883–1918 (New York: Columbia University Press, 2009), 159.

34. Hubert Henry Harrison. *Diary*. Columbia University Library Rare Book and Manuscripts Division. Box 9; folder 1. October 1907. The October entry is Harrison's first, but not last, discussion of the intentions to write and publish his work on Reconstruction in the South. Included in his correspondences are letters between him and Du Bois in which he asks Du Bois to suggest some books he may read to aid in his analysis of Black Reconstruction. Du Bois replies with some suggested works. Although Harrison gave several lectures on this topic, he never completed the book.

35. Hubert H. Harrison, *When Africa Awakes* (Baltimore, MD: Black Classic Press, 1997), 25.

36. Jervis Anderson, *A. Philip Randolph: A Biographical Portrait* (New York: Harcourt Brace Jovanovich, 1972), 104.

37. "Re: NEGRO AGITATION Socialist Activities" (November 1918), *UNIA Papers* 1: 291.

38. "The Conspiracy of the East St. Louis Riots," speech by Marcus Garvey (July 1917), *UNIA Papers* 1: 213.

39. "Re: Negro Agitation Marcus Garvey" (December 1918), *UNIA Papers* 1: 311.

40. "A New Radical Organization," printed in the *Afro American* (December 1918), *UNIA Papers* 1: 321.

41. "Address by Marcus Garvey in Brooklyn" (February 1919), *UNIA Papers* 1: 375.

42. Robert Hill, ed., *UNIA Papers* XI: cclxxv–cclxxvi.

43. Michael B. Katz, ed., *The "Underclass" Debate: Views from History*, essay by Joe William Trotter, Jr. "Blacks in the Urban North: The 'Underclass Question' in Historical Perspective," 68–69.

44. David M. Chalmers, *Hooded Americanism: The History of the Ku Klux Klan* (Durham, NC: Duke University Press, 1987), 26–27.

45. Ibid., 27.

46. See Edgerton, *Hidden Heroism*, 90–94.

47. W.E.B. Du Bois, "An Essay Toward a History of the Black Man in the Great War," *The Crisis* 18, no. 2 (June 1919): 87.

48. Ibid., 65.

49. Williams, *Torchbearers of Democracy*, 173.

50. Ibid.

51. It should be noted that the move towards collective racial pride based on common experiences in the World War I era was not relegated to the Black population. Mexican Americans and Mexican nationals, as well as the myriad American Indigenous groups who met each other overseas, also found a common space in which to understand their shared experiences of racial oppression. Many Latinos and American Indigenous overseas were limited in their ability to speak English and believed participation in the war would improve their status at home. The overwhelming majority had never left their respective homes in the American West or left the rural seclusion of the reservation. As a result, upon their return home, they discovered that their world views had changed and they gained a deep sense of Mexican or Indigenous pride, which leaned towards nationalism. Although this did not necessarily result in race riots amongst these groups, the emergence of this racial pride intersected with Black nationalism in the West in important ways.

52. Adam Ewing, "Caribbean Labour Politics in the Age of Garvey, 1918–1938," *Race and Class* 55, no. 1 (2013): 23, 28.

53. Robert Hill, *UNIA Papers* XI: ccxix.

54. See Martin, *Race First*; Robert Hill, ed. "Historical Commentaries," *UNIA Papers* XI.

55. Edgerton, *Hidden Heroism*, 109.

56. Ibid., 110.

57. Ibid.

58. Ronald Harpelle, "Cross Currents in the Western Caribbean,"

50.

59. Ewing, "Caribbean Labour Politics in the Age of Garvey," 28.

60. Ibid., 29.

61. Ibid., 30.

62. W. F. Elkins, "Black Power in the British West Indies: The Trinidad Longshoreman's Strike of 1919," *Science and Society* 33, no. 1 (Winter 1969): 73.

63. Ibid., 74.

64. Opie, "Garveyism and Labor Organization," 165.

65. Rolinson, *Grassroots Garveyism*, 86.

66. Ibid.

67. O. A. Rogers Jr., "The Elaine Race Riots of 1919," *The Arkansas Historical Quarterly* 19, no. 2 (Summer 1960): 144.

68. Rolinson, *Grassroots Garveyism*, 99.

69. *The Chicago Defender*, May 10, 1919, 10.

70. Ibid.

71. *The Chicago Defender*, October 4, 1919, 2.

72. Ibid.

73. Williams, *Torchbearers of Democracy*, 97.

CHAPTER 2

1. Quintard Taylor, *The Forging of a Black Community: Seattle's Central District from 1870 through the Civil Rights Era* (Seattle: University of Washington Press, 1994), 56.

2. Ibid, 52.

3. Anderson, *A. Philip Randolph*, 155.

4. Ibid., 158.

5. Ibid., 159.

6. Emory J. Tolbert. *The UNIA and Black Los Angeles Ideology and Community in the American Garvey movement.* Center for Afro-American Studies: University of California, Los Angeles, 1980, 31.

7. Ibid.

8. For Japanese, Filipino, and Chinese porters, see Larry Tye, *Rising from the Rails: Pullman Porters and the Rise of the Black Middle Class* (New York: Henry Holt and Company, 2004), 139–40. For Mexican porters see "Mexican Pullman [P]orters Threaten Strike," *The Black Worker* (Chicago, IL) 3, no. 1 (March 21, 1932), 3.

9. James Noble Gregory, *The Southern Diaspora: How the Great Migrations of Black and White Southerners Transformed America* (Chapel Hill: University of North Carolina Press, 2005), 14.

10. Ibid., 26.

11. Ibid., 27.

12. Redlining was a practice in which Blacks would be barred from purchasing homes outside of a "red line," which was drawn to reflect where Blacks or other racial groups could live.

13. Douglas Flamming, *Bound for Freedom: Black Los Angeles in Jim Crow America* (Berkeley: University of California Press, 2005), 219.

14. Darrell Millner, "The Color Line: Racial Discrimination in Portland, Oregon" (Portland: The Oregon Historical Society and the Central City Concern Association, Online Resource: http://www.centralcityconcern.org/goldenwest/colorlines.html).

15. Taylor, *The Forging of a Black Community*, 85.

16. Ibid.

17. For a more detailed account of discrimination faced by non-Black racial groups in the American West, see Mae M. Ngai, *Impossible Subjects: Illegal Aliens and the Making of Modern America* (Princeton, NJ: Princeton University Press, 2004).

18. Taylor, *The Forging of a Black Community*, 88.

19. Carlos M. Larralde and Richard Griswold del Castillo, "San Diego's Ku Klux Klan 1920–1980," *San Diego Historical*

Quarterly 46 (Spring/Summer 2000): 2–3.

20. William D. Carrigan and Clive Webb, *The Forgotten Dead: Mob Violence against Mexicans in the United States, 1848–1928* (New York: Oxford University Press, 2013), 121.

21. Ibid., 30.

22. Eckard Toy, "Ku Klux Klan," *The Oregon Encyclopedia*, A Project of the Oregon Historical Society.

23. Alton Hornsby Jr., ed., *Black America: A State-by-State Historical Encyclopedia*, vol. 2, Darrell Millner, "Oregon" (Santa Barbara: ABC-CLIO, 2011), 692.

24. Ibid, 692.

25. *Lynden Tribune*, October 1, 1925, 1.

26. Chalmers, *Hooded Americanism*, 119.

27. Ibid.

28. Tolbert, *UNIA in Black Los Angeles*, 31.

29. More information on the UNIA organizing in the South and their experiences with the KKK can be found in Rolinson, *Grassroots Garveyism*.

30. See Chalmers, *Hooded Americanism*, 122 and *UNIA Papers* 8: 987.

31. Taylor, *The Forging of a Black Community*, 90.

32. Tolbert, *UNIA in Black Los Angeles*, 89.

33. Ibid., 40.

34. Charlotta Bass (originally Charlotta Spears) was a well-known newspaper editor, educator, politician, and activist in early twentieth century Los Angeles. She sold issues of the *California Eagle*, Los Angeles' most widely read Black newspaper. When the newspaper's owner John Neimore died, Charlotta purchased the newspaper. She later married Joseph Bass, who became the paper's editor until his death in 1934. Charlotta kept the paper afloat until her own death in 1969.

35. Tolbert, *UNIA and Black Los Angeles*, 54.

36. Delilah L. Beasley, *The Negro Trailblazers of California* (San

Francisco, CA: California Historical Society 1968 [1919]), 255.

37. Report by Bureau Agents A. A. Hopkins and E. J. Kosterlitzky (February 19, 1921), *UNIA Papers* 3: 224.

38. Analyses that examine in great detail the divisions between Marcus Garvey and other Black leaders on the East Coast are well established in nearly every scholarly work on Garvey, including Tony Martin's *Race First*, Theodore Vincent's *Black Power and the Garvey Movement*, and Robert Hill's *UNIA Papers*, among others. Therefore, a discussion of Garvey's interactions with his enemies, such as W.E.B. Du Bois, Hubert Harrison, A. Philip Randolph, Cyril Briggs, and others will not be restated here in any great detail.

39. Vincent, *Garvey and the Black Power Movement*, 169.

40. Tolbert, *UNIA and Black Los Angeles*, 56.

41. Ibid., 60.

42. Ibid., 61.

43. Ibid.

44. What Emory Tolbert refers to as "Outpost Garveyism."

45. Vincent, *Black Power and the Garvey Movement*, 169.

46. Taylor, *The Forging of a Black Community*, 91.

47. Dearmon Jenkins, "Linking up the Golden Gate," 271.

48. Ibid.

49. Taylor, *The Forging of a Black Community*, 109.

50. Ibid., 57.

51. Marc Gallicchio, *The African American Encounter with Japan and China: Black Internationalism in Asia, 1895–1945* (Chapel Hill: University of North Carolina Press, 2000), 24.

52. "Report by Special Agent P-138" (October 22, 1920), *UNIA Papers* 3: 62.

53. "Report by Bureau Agent H.B. Pierce on Negro Activities" (April 25, 1921), *UNIA Papers* 3: 364.

54. National Archives, RG 38, no. 78: US Navy/Chief of Naval Operations/ Office of Naval Intelligence: [Formerly]

Confidential General Correspondences, Box 31, Weekly Report Japanese Activities, week ending March 18, 1922, 10.

55. Vincent, *Black Power and the Garvey Movement*, 171.

56. Seema Sohi, *Echoes of Mutiny: Race, Surveillance, and Indian Colonialism in North America* (New York: Oxford University Press, 2014), 21.

57. See Walton Look Lai, *Indentured Labor, Caribbean Sugar: Chinese and Indian Migrants to the British West Indies, 1838–1918* (Baltimore, MD: Johns Hopkins University Press, 2004).

58. Sohi, *Echoes of Mutiny*.

59. Ibid., 25.

60. "Hindoo Peril Rouses Mob: Foreign Mill Workers are Driven from Bellingham, Wash." *Chicago Daily Tribune*, September 6, 1907, 5.

61. Ibid.

62. Sohi, *Echoes of Mutiny*, 46.

63. Ibid.

64. Ibid., 56.

65. See Gerald Horne's *The End of Empires* for a more expansive account of Black interactions with Indians in the United States.

66. Quoted in Erika Lee and Judy Yung, *Angel Island: Immigrant Gateway to America* (New York: Oxford University Press 2010), 149.

67. Sohi, *Echoes of Mutiny*, 61.

68. Ibid., 57.

69. Ibid., 153.

70. Ibid.

71. Ibid., 202.

72. National Archives, RG 38, no. 78: US Navy/Chief of Naval Operations/Office of Naval Intelligence: [Formerly] Confidential General Correspondences, Box 31, ID 20964; Weekly Report Japanese Activities (week ending February 4, 1922), 8.

73. Ibid.

74. Ibid., RDW F. Morse (week ending March 18, 1922), 11.

75. "J. J. Hannigan, Commandant, Twelfth Naval District, to the Director, Office of Naval Intelligence (December 3, 1921), *UNIA Papers* 4: 236.

76. Ibid.

77. National Archives, RG 38, no. 78: US Navy/Chief of Naval Operations/ Office of Naval Intelligence: [Formerly] Confidential General Correspondences, Box 31,ID 20964; Weekly Report Japanese Activities (week ending 4 March 1922), 2.

78. It is important to note that legally, Mexicans were defined as white. Yet, they are included here as part of the experience of people of color because they did not enjoy the same rights as whites of European descent.

79. Zimmerman Telegram (decoded) National Archives and Records Administration, RG 59, General Records of the Department of State, 1756–1979, ID 302022.

80. Friedrich Katz, *The Secret War in Mexico: Europe, the United States, and the Mexican Revolution* (Chicago: University of Chicago Press, 1981), 303.

81. For a thorough discussion of the life of Pershing's experience with Black soldiers see Frank Everson Vandiver, *Black Jack: The Life and Times of John J. Pershing*, vol. 1 (College Station: Texas A&M University Press, 1977).

82. Carrigan and Webb, *The Forgotten Dead*, 85.

83. Ibid., 23.

84. Katz, *The Secret War in Mexico*, 514.

85. Britten, *American Indians in World War I*, 122.

86. Ibid., 123.

87. Lawrence B. de Graaf, Kevin Mulroy, and Quintard Taylor, eds. *Seeking El Dorado: African Americans in California* (Seattle: University of Washington Press, 2001), 159.

88. Britten, *American Indians in World War I*, 123.

89. Nicolás Kanellos and Claudio Esteva-Fabregat, ed., *Handbook of Hispanic Culture in the United States*, 47.

90. Vincent, *Black Power and the Garvey Movement*, 170.

91. Ibid., 170–71.

92. See Carrigan and Webb, *The Forgotten Dead*.

93. Although evidence of funding sent to aid the colony has not been found, for further information regarding this letter, see *UNIA Papers* 3: 321–22.

94. de Graaf et al., *Seeking El Dorado*, 161.

95. To read more about early Japanese immigration to Mexico see: Selfa A. Chew, *Uprooting Community: Japanese Mexicans, World War II, and the US Mexico Borderlands* (Tucson: University of Arizona Press, 2015).

96. National Archives, RG 38, no. 78: US Navy/Chief of Naval Operations/Office of Naval Intelligence: [Formerly] Confidential General Correspondences, Box 31, ID 20964 (March 1922).

97. Ibid.

98. Sarah Schrank, *Art and the City: Civic Imagination and Cultural Authority in Los Angeles* (Philadelphia: University of Pennsylvania Press, 2009), 73.

CHAPTER 3

1. Although UNIA members created other economic ventures, such as UNIA laundromats, restaurants, a printing press, etc., this chapter focuses solely on the BSL as an economic possibility for independence. Unlike the other business ventures, which were local businesses that primarily benefited the Black residents in Harlem, New York, the BSL represented a global path to economic freedom and stood to benefit the Black 365 diaspora.

2. John McCartney, *Black Power Ideologies: An Essay in African*

American Political Thought (Philadelphia, PA: Temple University Press, 1993), 29–30.

3. A deeper discussion of this shipping line comes later in the chapter.

4. Grant, *Negro with A Hat*, 206.

5. Robert Hill, *UNIA Papers* 1: xlvii.

6. Abraham Berglund, "Our Merchant Marine Problem and International Trade Policies," *Journal of Political Economy* 34, no. 5 (October 1926): 644.

7. Paul Wood, "The History of Elder Dempster," *Rakaia* (2006).

8. Laura Tabili, "'Keeping the Natives under Control': Race Segregation and the Domestic Dimensions of Empire, 1920–1930," *International Labor and Working-Class History*, no. 44 (Fall 1993): 64–65.

9. Robert Hill, ed. *The Marcus Garvey and Universal Negro Improvement Papers: Africa for the Africans June 1921–1922*, vol. IX (Berkeley: University of California Press 1995), xlvii.

10. Casper W. Erichsen, *The Angel of Death has Descended Violently among Them: Concentration Camps and Prisoners-of-War in Namibia, 1904–1908* (Leiden: African Studies Center 2005), 23.

11. Adam Hochschild, *King Leopold's Ghost: A Story of Greed, Terror, and Heroism in Colonial Africa* (New York: Houghton Mifflin Company), 233.

12. Ibid., 209–24.

13. Ayodeji Olukoju, "Elder Dempster and the Shipping Trade of Nigeria during the First World War," *The Journal of African History* 33, no. 2 (1992): 258.

14. Michael Kasongo, *History of the Methodist Church in the Central Congo* (Lanham, MD: University Press of America, 1998), 46.

15. See Mhoze Chikowero, *African Music, Power, and Being in Colonial Zimbabwe* for a detailed account of the complex

colonial processes and resistance movements in Southern Rhodesia (Zimbabwe).

16. West, "The Seeds are Sown," 341.

17. Ibid., 343.

18. C. D. B., "Captain Joshua Cockburn," *The Lagos Weekly Record* (Lagos, Nigeria), September 13, 1919, 3.

19. "The Republic of Africa," *The Colonial and Provincial Reporter* (Freetown, Sierra Leone), October 2, 1920, 9.

20. "To the Editor of the Times of Nigeria," *The Times of Nigeria* (Lagos, Nigeria), May 24, 1920, 4.

21. T. S. Sanjeeva Rao, *A Short History of Modern Indian Shipping* (Bombay: Popular Prakashan, 1965), 40.

22. Ibid., 78.

23. Ibid., 92.

24. Mahatma Gandhi began his movement of civil disobedience in the Indian community of South Africa. He later moved to India and led movements there against excessive taxation, the caste system, colonial rule, and other rights abuses. His nonviolent movement was an inspiration to later civil rights era leaders, such as Martin Luther King Jr.

25. Rao, *A Short History of Modern Indian Shipping*, 92.

26. Mark Moberg, "Crown Colony as Banana Republic: The United Fruit Company in British Honduras, 1900–1920," *Journal of Latin American Studies* 28, no. 2 (May 1996): 366.

27. Ibid.

28. Ibid.

29. "Bureau of Investigation Report: Negro Activities and the Black Star Line," (May 28, 1919) *UNIA Papers* 1: 412.

30. Ibid., 413–14.

31. Tolbert, *UNIA in Los Angeles*, 52.

32. Taylor, *The Forging of a Black Community*, 55.

33. Ibid., 58.

34. Albert S. Broussard, *Black San Francisco: The Struggle for*

Racial Equality in the West, 1900–1954 (Lawrence: University Press of Kansas, 1993).

35. Dearmon Jenkins, "Linking Up the Golden Gate," 274.

36. Ibid., 273.

37. Ibid., 275.

38. Ibid.

39. Ibid., 274.

40. Douglas Henry Daniels, *Pioneer Urbanites: A Social and Cultural History of Black San Francisco* (Berkeley: University of California Press, 1900), 82.

41. Dearmon Jenkins, "Linking Up the Golden Gate," 274.

42. Garvey had established the UNIA in Jamaica seven years earlier in 1914, and by 1919 it had become widely popular throughout the Caribbean.

43. Dana Frank, "Race Relations and the Seattle Labor Movement, 1915–1929," *The Pacific Northwest Quarterly* 86, no. 1 (Winter, 1994/1995), 36.

44. Ibid., 38.

45. Ibid.

46. Martin, *Race First*, 96.

47. Quintard Taylor, "Blacks and Asians in a White City: Japanese Americans and African Americans in Seattle, 1890–1940," *Western Historical Quarterly* 22, no. 4 (November 1991): 426.

48. Gerald Horne, *Red Seas: Ferdinand Smith and the Radical Black Sailors in the United States and Jamaica* (New York: New York University Press, 2005), 17.

49. Ibid.

50. Martin, *Race First*, 152.

51. "US Plans to Jim Crow the Ocean," *The Advocate*, March 1, 1930.

52. Mrs. Mabel Johnson, "Mothers of Heroes Pained Over Gov't Treatment," *The Advocate*, June 28, 1930.

53. Ibid.

54. "Report by Bureau Agent H.B. Pierce" (April 25, 1921), *UNIA Papers* 3: 364.

55. Martin, *Race First*, 164.

56. Ibid., 166.

57. Ibid.

58. Taylor, *The Veiled Garvey*, 3.

59. Michael Ezra, ed., *Civil Rights Movement: People and Perspectives*, "Black Nationalists" by Yusuf Nurddin (Santa Barbara: ABC-CLIO, Inc., 2009), 99.

60. Adam Ewing, *The Age of Garvey: How a Jamaican Activist Created a Mass Movement and Changed Global Black Politics* (Princeton, NJ: Princeton University Press, 2014), 108.

61. Quoted in Robert Eric Barde, *Immigration at the Golden Gate* (Westport, CT: Praeger Publishers 2008), 154.

62. Congress created and funded the US Shipping Board during World War I after a German submarine sank the English passenger ship *Lusitania* and as shipping dwindled and affected the transportation of goods. The US Shipping Board created the Emergency Fleet Corporation, which built ships and appropriated and repaired German ships confiscated in war.

63. Ibid., 174.

64. "Robert P. Stewart, Assistant Attorney General, to William Bauchop Wilson, Secretary of Labor," Washington, DC (August 15, 1919), *UNIA Papers* 1: 482–83.

65. Ramla M. Bandele, *Black Star: African American Activism in the International Political Economy* (Champaign: University of Illinois Press, 2008), 103.

66. Ibid., 52.

67. "Memorandum from the Office of the Governor-General of French West Africa," *UNIA Papers* 9: 363.

68. Robert Hill and Barbara Blair, ed. *Marcus Garvey Life and Lessons* (Berkeley: University of California Press, 1987), 370.

69. Judith Stein, *The World of Marcus Garvey*, 91.

70. Bendele, *Black Star*, 145.

71. Hugh Mulzac, *A Star to Steer By* (New York: New York International Publishers, 1963), 78.

72. Ibid.

73. Cronon, *Black Moses*, 84.

74. Martin, *Race First*, 163–64.

75. "Fifth Annual Report of the United States Shipping Board" (Washington, DC: Government Printing Office, 1921), 18.

76. Ibid., 63.

77. Tolbert, *UNIA and Black Los Angeles*, 21.

78. Cronon, *Black Moses*, 88.

79. Grant, *Negro with A Hat*, 292.

80. "Speech by Marcus Garvey" (July 1921), *UNIA Papers* 3: 537.

81. None of Garvey's ships ever made it to Africa.

82. C. F. Simmons, "The 1921 Tulsa Race Riot," *The Crisis* (July 1921): 18.

83. Bandele, *Black Star*, 115.

84. Cronon, *Black Moses*, 92.

85. Herbert Aptheker and Fay Aptheker, "Personal Reflections on W.E.B. Du Bois," in *Against the Odds: Scholars Who Challenged Racism in the Twentieth Century*, Benjamin P. Bowser and Louis Kushnick, eds. (Amherst: University of Massachusetts Press 2002), 175.

86. *Marcus Garvey v. United States*, US Circuit Court of Appeals, Second Circuit (New York, December 15, 1924) *UNIA Papers* VI: 72–73.

87. Cronon, *Black Moses*, 121.

88. Quoted in Grant, *Negro with a Hat*, 204.

89. Herbert Aptheker, *The Correspondence of W.E.B. DuBois* (Amherst: University of Massachusetts Press, 1973), 261.

CHAPTER 4

1. *California Eagle* (Los Angeles), October 29, 1921, 1.

2. "The Black Star Line," [letter from Ella Ross Hurston] Printed in *The Crisis* (September 1922), *UNIA Papers* 5: 41.

3. Tolbert, *UNIA and Black Los Angeles*, 67.

4. "Progressives Quit Marcus Garvey," *California Eagle*, November 21, 1921, 1.

5. Quoted in Quintard Taylor and Shirley Ann Wilson Moore, eds., *African American Women Confront the West, 1600–2000* (Norman: University of Oklahoma Press, 2003), 204–5.

6. Speech by Marcus Garvey (Liberty Hall, July 4, 1922), *UNIA Papers* 4: 692.

7. Ibid., 693.

8. "J. J. Hannigan, to the Director, Office of Naval Intelligence" (San Francisco, June 19, 1922), *UNIA Papers* 4: 678.

9. Dearmon Jenkins, "Linking Up the Golden Gate," 268.

10. Ibid., 670.

11. "Report by Bureau Agents A. A. Hopkins and E. J. Kosterlitzky" (Los Angeles, February 10, 1921), *UNIA Papers* 3: 176.

12. Freedom of Information and Privacy Acts, *Marcus Garvey*, FN 190–1781-6, FBI, 4.

13. See Grant, *Negro with a Hat*.

14. Chalmers, *Hooded Americanism*, 202.

15. Sara Bullard, ed., *The Ku Klux Klan: A History of Racism and Violence* (Montgomery, AL: Southern Poverty Law Center, 1997), 19.

16. "Will Stand by Slogan: Africa for the Africans at Home and Abroad!" (September 7, 1921), *UNIA Papers* 9: 187.

17. There were more UNIA chapters in the South than any other part of the country. Louisiana alone had seventy-four chapters by 1926. A comparison of Klan chapter locations and UNIA chapter locations in this region reveals that the two organizations were often established very near each other in the same towns. For example, in Elaine, Arkansas, where the largest race

riot in that state's history occurred, there were thirty UNIA chapters within a fifty-mile radius of the town. One reason so many chapters could exist in such a hostile environment was that southern Garveyites, like the Klan, heavily promoted segregation of the races. For an excellent discussion of Garveyism in the American South, see Rolinson, *Grassroots Garveyism*.

18. Grant, *Negro with a Hat*, 335.
19. Ibid., 333.
20. "Letter from KKK to Marcus Garvey" (June 26, 1923) US District Court for the Southern District of New York. National Archives and Records Administration. Case #RG 276, 8317. Archives Box # 2816.
21. Quoted in Grant, *Negro with a Hat*, 333.
22. Ibid.
23. P. Solomon Banda, "Meeting of NAACP chapter and KKK organizer in Wyoming believed to be first," Associated Press, September 2, 2013.
24. "Hon. Marcus Garvey Tells of Interview with Ku Klux Klan" (Liberty Hall, July 9, 1922), *UNIA Papers* 4: 707.
25. See Anderson, *A. Philip Randolph*.
26. Quoted in Tolbert, *UNIA and Black Los Angeles*, 70.
27. The California Supreme Court in 1948 struck down the anti-miscegenation law in *Perez v. Sharp*. Andrea Perez, who was Mexican, wanted to marry Sylvester Davis, who was Black. As a Mexican woman, Perez was considered white. Ironically, they used the defense that because the Catholic Church was willing to marry them, regardless of their race, that the state was violating their Constitutional right to practice religion. The California Supreme Court agreed by a majority of one vote and California became the first state to repeal its anti-miscegenation laws which had been on the books since it became a state in 1850. See Robin A. Lenhardt, "Perez v. Sharp and the Limits of Loving," in Kevin Noble Maillard and Rose

Cuison Villazor, eds., *In a Post-Racial World: Rethinking Race, Sex, and Marriage* (New York: Cambridge University Press 2012), 73.

28. Phyl Newbeck, *Virginia Hasn't Always Been for Lovers: Interracial Intermarriage Bans and the Case of Richard and Mildred Loving* (Carbondale: Southern Illinois University, 2004), 101.

29. Tolbert, *UNIA and Black Los Angeles*, 71.

30. Ibid., 70.

31. Ibid., 71.

32. *California Eagle*, September 2, 1922, 1.

33. "Los Angeles," *California Eagle*, September 2, 1922, 1.

34. J. J. Hannigan to the Director, Office of Naval Intelligence, "Gandhi and Garvey" (February 4, 1922) *UNIA Papers* 4: 477.

35. Gallicchio, *The African American Encounter with Japan and China*, 43–44.

36. Quoted in Sohi, *Echoes of Mutiny*, 202.

37. See Roger Daniels, *The Politics of Prejudice: The Anti-Japanese Movement in California and the Struggle for Japanese Exclusion* (Berkeley: University of California Press, 1999).

38. Gallicchio, *The African American Encounter with Japan and China*, 53.

39. Ibid.

40. Tolbert, *UNIA and Black Los Angeles*, 81.

41. Ibid., 81.

42. His derogatory term for people who wore turbans—most likely South Asians from India.

43. Hugh Carey McWilliams, *Factories in the Fields: The Story of Migratory Farm Labor in California* (Boston, MA: Little, Brown, and Co., 1939. Reprinted with new index added, Berkeley: University of California Press, 1966), 104–34.

44. See Quintard Taylor, "Black Towns," *Encyclopedia of African American Culture and History*, 2nd ed., vol. 1. Colin A. Palmer,

ed., *Macmillan Reference USA* (2006).

45. See Gary R. Entz, "Benjamin Pap Singleton: Father of the Kansas Exodus," in *Portraits of African American Life since 1865*, Nina Mjagkij, ed. (Wilmington, DE: Scholarly Resources, Inc., 2003).

46. Daniel Geisseler and William R. Horwath, "Cotton Production in California," prepared within the project "Assessment of Plant Fertility and Fertilizer Requirements for Agricultural Crops in California," funded by the California Department of Food and Agriculture Fertilizer Research and Education Program (February 2013), 1.

47. Devra Weber, *Dark Sweat, White Gold: California Farmworkers, Cotton, and the New Deal* (Berkeley, CA: University of California Press, 1994), 23.

48. See Michael Eissinger, "Growing Along the Side of the Road: Rural African American Settlements in Central California," unpublished essay presented at *Horizons of Change: The Unexpected, Unknown, and Unfortunate, Annual Meeting of the Pacific Coast Branch of the American Historical Association*, Seattle, August 2011.

49. de Graaf et al., *Seeking El Dorado*, 153.

50. Harold Cruse, *The Crisis of the Negro Intellectual: A Historical Analysis of the Failure of Black Leadership* (New York: New York Review Books, 1967), 426.

51. Beasley, *The Negro Trail Blazers of California*, 154.

52. Quoted in de Graaf et al., *Seeking El Dorado*, 154.

53. Ibid.

54. Quoted in Mickey Ellinger, "Allensworth Freedom Colony: An Experiment in African American Self-Determination," *Race, Poverty, and the Environment* (Spring 2009): 28.

55. Ibid., 29.

56. Alice C. Royal, Mickey Ellinger, and Scott Braley. *Allensworth, the Freedom Colony: A California African American Township*

(Berkeley, CA: Heyday Institute, 2008), 63.

57. Ibid., 29.

58. Quoted in ibid., *Allensworth, the Freedom Colony*, 39.

59. Ibid., 60.

60. Ibid., 47.

61. Quoted in Richard Steven Street, *Beasts of the Field: A Narrative History of California Farmworkers, 1769–1913* (Stanford, CA: Stanford University Press, 2004), 491.

62. Ibid.

63. Ibid., 492.

64. Benny J. Andres, *Power and Control in the Imperial Valley: Nature, Agribusiness, and Workers on the California Borderland 1900–1940* (College Station: Texas A&M University Press, 2014), 100.

65. Sohi, *Echoes of Mutiny.*

66. Ibid., 178.

67. Ibid., 208.

68. Robin Kelley, *Race Rebels: Culture, Politics, and the Black Working Class* (New York: Free Press, 1994), 106–7; Alphonso Pinkney, *Red, Black, and Green: Black Nationalism in the United States* (Cambridge, UK: Cambridge University Press, 1976), 58.

69. Martin, *Race First*, 252.

70. Ibid., 253.

71. Leslie James, *George Padmore and Decolonization from Below: Pan-Africanism, the Cold War, and the End of Empire* (New York: Palgrave Macmillan 2015), 28.

72. W.E.B. Du Bois, *The Crisis: A Record of the Darker Races*, vol. 61, December–January 1954, "The Problem of Communist Affiliation," Alfred Baker Lewis (New York: Anno Press 1969), 585–88.

73. Josh Sides, *L. A. City Limits: African American Los Angeles from the Great Depression to the Present* (Berkeley: University of

California Press, 2003), 32.

74. Ibid.

75. Hakim Adi, *Pan-Africanism and Communism: The Communist International, Africa and the Diaspora, 1919–1939* (Trenton, NJ: Africa World Press, 2013), 175.

76. George Padmore, "Ethiopia and World Politics," *The Crisis* (May 1935): 138.

77. Adi, *Pan-Africanism and Communism*, 180.

78. See George M. Beckmann and Okubo Genji, *The Japanese Communist Party 1922–1945* (Stanford, CA: Stanford University Press, 1969).

CONCLUSION

1. Sohi, *Echoes of Mutiny*, 202.

2. Lee and Yung, *Angel Island*, 4.

3. Gallicchio, *The African American Encounter with Japan and China*, 50.

4. "The Chinese Poisoned Against the Japanese," speech at Olympia Theater, November 1921, *UNIA Papers* 4: 186.

5. Grant, *Negro with a Hat*, 277.

6. For Ghana's shipping line see Yitzhak Oran, ed., *Middle East Record*, vol. 1 (London, UK: George Weidenfeld and Nicolson Limited), 310; for Black Star Credit Union see: http://www.blackstarlinecooperativecreditunion.com/

7. Cronon, *Black Moses*, 78.

8. Weber, *Dark Sweat, White Gold*, 99.

9. Ibid.

10. Stephanie Lewthwaite, *Race, Place and Reform in Mexican Los Angeles: A Transnational Perspective, 1890–1940* (Tucson: University of Arizona Press, 2009), 164.

BIBLIOGRAPHY

Adi, Hakim. *Pan-Africanism and Communism: The Communist International, Africa and the Diaspora, 1919–1939.* Trenton, NJ: Africa World Press, 2013.

Anderson, Jervis. *A. Philip Randolph: A Biographical Portrait.* New York: Harcourt Brace Jovanovich, 1972.

Andres, Benny J. *Power and Control in the Imperial Valley: Nature, Agribusiness, and Workers on the California Borderland 1900–1940.* College Station: Texas A&M University Press, 2014.

Aptheker, Herbert, ed. *The Correspondence of W.E.B. DuBois.* Amherst: University of Massachusetts Press, 1973.

Bandele, Ramla M. *Black Star: African American Activism in the International Political Economy.* Champaign: University of Illinois Press, 2008.

Beasley, Delilah L. *The Negro Trailblazers of California.* San Francisco, CA: California Historical Society 1968 [1919].

Beckmann, George M., and Okubo Genji. *The Japanese Communist Party 1922–1945.* Stanford, CA: Stanford University Press, 1969.

Britten, Thomas A. *American Indians in World War I: At Home and at War.* Albuquerque: University of New Mexico Press, 1997.

Broussard, Albert S. *Black San Francisco: The Struggle for Racial Equality in the West, 1900–1954.* Lawrence: University Press of Kansas, 1993.

Bullard, Sara, ed. *The Ku Klux Klan: A History of Racism and Violence.* Montgomery, AL: Southern Poverty Law Center, 1997.

Carrigan, William D., and Clive Webb. *The Forgotten Dead: Mob Violence against Mexicans in the United States, 1848–1928.* New York: Oxford University Press, 2013.

Chalmers, David M. *Hooded Americanism: The History of the Ku Klux Klan.* Durham, NC: Duke University Press, 1987.

Chikowero, Mhoze. *African Music, Power, and Being in Colonial Zimbabwe.* Bloomington: Indiana University Press, 2015.

Clarke, John Henrik. *Marcus Garvey and the Vision of Africa.* New York: Vintage Books, 1974.

Colby, Jason M. *The Business of Empire: United Fruit, Race, and the U.S. Expansion in Central America.* Ithaca, NY: Cornell University Press, 2011.

Cronon, E. David. *Black Moses: The Story of Marcus Garvey and the Universal Negro Improvement Association.* Madison: University of Wisconsin Press, 1955 and 1969.

Cruse, Harold. *The Crisis of the Negro Intellectual: A Historical Analysis of the Failure of Black Leadership.* New York: New York Review Books, 1967.

Daniels, Douglas Henry. *Pioneer Urbanites: A Social and Cultural History of Black San Francisco.* Berkeley: University of California Press, 1900.

Daniels, Roger. *The Politics of Prejudice: The Anti-Japanese Movement in California and the Struggle for Japanese Exclusion.* Berkeley: University of California Press, 1999.

de Graaf, Lawrence B., Kevin Mulroy, and Quintard Taylor, eds. *Seeking El Dorado: African Americans in California.* Seattle: University of Washington Press, 2001.

Dearmon Jenkins, Robin. "Linking Up the Golden Gate." *Journal of Black Studies* 39, no. 2 (2008), 266–80.

Edgerton, Robert B. *Hidden Heroism: Black Soldiers in America's Wars.* Boulder, CO: Westview Press, 2002.

Ewing, Adam. *The Age of Garvey: How a Jamaican Activist Created a Mass Movement and Changed Global Black Politics.* Princeton, NJ: Princeton University Press, 2014.

Flamming, Douglas. *Bound for Freedom: Black Los Angeles in Jim Crow America.* Berkeley: University of California Press, 2005.

Gallicchio, Marc. *The African American Encounter with Japan and China: Black Internationalism in Asia, 1895–1945.* Chapel Hill: University of North Carolina Press, 2000.

Garvey, Amy Jacques, ed. *Philosophy and Opinions of Marcus Garvey.* University Publishing House, 1923. (Reprinted with new preface 1925.) Dover, MA: The Majority Press, 1986.

Grant, Colin. *Negro with a Hat: The Rise and Fall of Marcus Garvey.* New York: Oxford University Press, 2008.

Greene, Helen Taylor, and Shaun L. Gabbidon, eds. *Encyclopedia of Race and Crime.* Thousand Oaks, CA: Sage, 2009.

Gregory, James Noble. *The Southern Diaspora: How the Great Migrations of Black and White Southerners Transformed America.* Chapel Hill: University of North Carolina Press, 2005.

Harrison, Hubert H. *When Africa Awakes.* Baltimore, MD: Black Classic Press, 1997.

Hernández, Tanya Katerí. *Racial Subordination in Latin America: The Role of the State, Customary Law, and the New Civil Rights Response.* New York: Cambridge University Press, 2013.

Higman, B. W. *A Concise History of the Caribbean.* New York: Cambridge University Press, 2011.

Horne, Gerald. *The End of Empires: African Americans and India.* Philadelphia, PA: Temple University Press, 2008.

———. *Red Seas: Ferdinand Smith and the Radical Black Sailors in the United States and Jamaica.* New York: New York University Press, 2005.

Hornsby, Alton, Jr., ed., *Black America: A State-by-State Historical Encyclopedia*, vol. 2. Santa Barbara: ABC-CLIO, 2011.

Kanellos, Nicolás, and Claudio Esteva-Fabregat, eds., *Handbook*

159

of Hispanic Culture in the United States: Anthropology. Houston, TX: Arte Público Press, 1994.

Kasongo, Michael. *History of the Methodist Church in the Central Congo.* Lanham, MD: University Press of America, 1998.

Katz, Friedrich. *The Secret War in Mexico: Europe, the United States, and the Mexican Revolution.* Chicago: University of Chicago Press, 1981.

Katz, Michael B., ed. *The "Underclass" Debate: Views from History.* Princeton, NJ: Princeton University Press, 1993.

Kelley, Robin. *Race Rebels: Culture, Politics, and the Black Working Class.* New York: Free Press, 1994.

Lai, Walton Look. *Indentured Labor, Caribbean Sugar: Chinese and Indian Migrants to the British West Indies, 1838–1918.* Baltimore, MD: Johns Hopkins University Press, 2004.

Lee, Erika, and Judy Yung. *Angel Island: Immigrant Gateway to America.* New York: Oxford University Press, 2010.

Lewthwaite, Stephanie. *Race, Place and Reform in Mexican Los Angeles: A Transnational Perspective, 1890–1940.* Tucson: University of Arizona Press, 2009.

Marable, Manning, and Leith Mullings, eds. *Let Nobody Turn Us Around: Voices of Resistance, Reform, and Renewal.* Lanham, MD: Rowman and Littlefield Publishers, 2000.

Martin, Tony. *Race First: The Ideological and Organizational Struggles of Marcus Garvey and the Universal Negro Improvement Association.* Dover, MA: The Majority Press, 1976.

McCartney, John. *Black Power Ideologies: An Essay in African American Political Thought.* Philadelphia, PA: Temple University Press, 1993.

McWilliams, Hugh Carey. *Factories in the Fields: The Story of Migratory Farm Labor in California.* Boston, MA: Little, Brown, and Co., 1939. Reprinted with new index added, Berkeley: University of California Press, 1966.

Mjagkij, Nina, ed. *Portraits of African American Life since 1865.*

Wilmington, DE: Scholarly Resources, Inc., 2003.

Mulzac, Hugh. *A Star to Steer By.* New York: New York International Publishers, 1963.

Newbeck, Phyl. *Virginia Hasn't Always Been for Lovers: Interracial Intermarriage Bans and the Case of Richard and Mildred Loving.* Carbondale: Southern Illinois University, 2004.

Newton, Michael. *White Robes and Burning Crosses: A History of the Ku Klux Klan from 1866.* Jefferson, NC: McFarland and Company, Inc., 2014.

Ngai, Mae M. *Impossible Subjects: Illegal Aliens and the Making of Modern America.* Princeton, NJ: Princeton University Press 2004.

Nuruddin, Yusuf. "Black Nationalists." In *Civil Rights Movement: People and Perspectives,* edited by Michael Ezra, Santa Barbara, CA: ABC-CLIO, Inc., 2009.

Osofsky, Gilbert. *Harlem: The Making of a Ghetto.* New York: Harper Torchbooks, 1963.

Pérez, Louis A, Jr. *Cuba and the United States: Ties of Singular Intimacy.* Athens: University of Georgia Press, 2003.

Perry, Jeffrey. *Hubert Harrison: The Voice of Harlem Radicalism, 1883–1918.* New York: Columbia University Press, 2009.

Pinkney, Alphonso. *Red, Black, and Green: Black Nationalism in the United States.* Cambridge, UK: Cambridge University Press, 1976.

Rao, T. S. Sanjeeva. *A Short History of Modern Indian Shipping.* Bombay: Popular Prakashan, 1965.

Rolinson, Mary G. *Grassroots Garveyism: The Universal Negro Improvement Association in the Rural South 1920–1927.* Chapel Hill: University of North Carolina Press, 2007.

Rosales, Arturo. *Chicano! The History of the Mexican American Civil Rights Movement.* Houston, TX: Arte Público Press, 1996.

Royal, Alice C., Mickey Ellinger, and Scott Braley. *Allensworth, the Freedom Colony: A California African American Township.*

Berkeley, CA: Heyday Institute, 2008.

Schrank, Sarah. *Art and the City: Civic Imagination and Cultural Authority in Los Angeles*. Philadelphia: University of Pennsylvania Press, 2009.

Sides, Josh. *L. A. City Limits: African American Los Angeles from the Great Depression to the Present*. Berkeley: University of California Press, 2003.

Smith, Robert. *Encyclopedia of African-American Politics*. Trenton, NJ: VB Hermitage, 2003.

Sohi, Seema. *Echoes of Mutiny: Race, Surveillance, and Indian Colonialism in North America*. New York: Oxford University Press, 2014.

Stein, Judith. *The World of Marcus Garvey: Race and Class in Modern Society*. Baton Rouge: Louisiana State University Press, 1986.

Street, Richard Steven. *Beasts of the Field: A Narrative History of California Farmworkers, 1769–1913*. Stanford, CA: Stanford University Press, 2004.

Taylor, Quintard. *The Forging of a Black Community: Seattle's Central District from 1870 through the Civil Rights Era*. Seattle: University of Washington Press, 1994.

Taylor, Quintard, and Shirley Ann Wilson Moore, eds. *African American Women Confront the West, 1600–2000*. Norman: University of Oklahoma Press, 2003.

Taylor, Ula. *The Veiled Garvey: Life and Times of Amy Jacques Garvey*. Chapel Hill: University of North Carolina Press, 2002.

Tolbert, Emory J. *The UNIA and Black Los Angeles: Ideology and Community in the American Garvey Movement*. Center for Afro-American Studies: University of California, Los Angeles, 1980.

Vandiver, Frank Everson. *Black Jack: The Life and Times of John J. Pershing*, vol. 1. College Station: Texas A&M University Press, 1977.

Villazor, Maillard, and Rose Cuison Villazor, eds. *In a Post-Racial World: Rethinking Race, Sex, and Marriage.* New York: Cambridge University Press, 2012.

Vincent, Theodore G. *Black Power and the Garvey Movement.* Berkeley, CA: The Ramparts Press, 1970.

Weber, Devra. *Dark Sweat, White Gold: California Farmworkers, Cotton, and the New Deal.* Berkeley, CA: University of California Press, 1994.

Williams, Chad L. *Torchbearers of Democracy: African American Soldiers in World War I Era.* Chapel Hill: University of North Carolina Press, 2010.

Woodward, C. Vann. *The Strange Career of Jim Crow.* New York: Oxford University Press, 1974.

INDEX

Adams, J. J., 54
The Advocate (Portland, Oregon), 82

Africa
 Back to Africa movement, 61, 65–66, 73–74, 93
 black soldiers in, 22
 Garveyism in, 73–74
 German West Africa, 70
 Liberia in, 61, 86, 92, 93
African Interland Missionary Society, 67
African Legion, 31, 124
African National Congress of South Africa, 73
African Times and Orient Review, xiv, 9
Afro-American Steamship and Mercantile Company, 66
Agent 800, 31–32. *See also* James (Wormley) Jones
Allensworth, California, 109, 111–14, 129
Allensworth, Allen, 112
American Federation of Labor, 80
Angel Island, 125
anti-lynching, 103

Ashwood, Amy, xiv
Asiatic Exclusion League, 36, 51, 125

Bakersfield, California, 41, 109, 111, 129
Baltimore Afro-American, 108
Bass, Charlotta, 43, 62, 95, 104, 106
Benefit Society, 72
Birth of A Nation, 20–21
Black Cross Nurses, 31, 93, 97, 124
Black nationalism, xx, xxi, 33, 45, 114, 123, 130
Black nationalist movement, xix, xxiii, 3, 9, 18–19, 118, 120
Black nationalists, xxii, 109, 120, 126, 129
 and India, 50, 54, 63, 107, 117
 and Mexico, 36, 40, 59, 62–63
Black regiments, 12–14, 21 58
Black Star Line, xix, xxi, 48, 65, 77, 86
 and Africa, 73–74, 84
 and Central America, 84, 89–90

creation of, 67–68
decline of, 93–94
legacy of, 127
Black Cross Navigation and
  Trading Company, 93
Briggs, Cyril, xvi, 44
British West Indian Regiment,
  19
Brotherhood of Sleeping Car
  Porters, 104
Brown v. Board of Education, 5
Buffalo Soldiers, 58, 112
Bureau of Investigation, 31,
  60–61, 76, 92–93, 103

California, xvii, 35–37, 39,
  41, 105, 108, 111–13, 119,
  127–29
    Asiatic Exclusion League,
      51
    Garvey visit, 109
    Indian nationalism, 50
    labor organizing, 46
    and Mexico, 59–62, 110,
      115
    UNIA, 43, 46, 49, 62, 83,
      96, 104
California Colony and Home
  Promoting Association, 112
California Eagle, 43, 62, 96, 106
Caribbean, 5–6, 10, 18, 22–25,
  32, 66, 124–25
    Black Star Line, 72, 126
    Garvey in, xiv
    labor movements in,
      26–28
    UFC in, 6–7, 75–76
Central America, 46, 52, 93

UFC in, 6–7, 75–76
UNIA in, 77
China Mail Steamship
  Company, 85–86
Civil War, 3, 5, 19–20, 102, 105,
  112
Clansman, The (Dixon), 20
Clarke, Edward Young, 99,
  101–2
Cockburn, Joshua, 87
colonialism, 36, 48, 50, 53, 69,
  93, 125
Communist Party (CPUSA),
  118–19, 129–30
    Costa Rica, 24`
    Garvey in, 7, 9, 90–91
    UFC in, 8, 75, 90
The Crisis, 15, 21, 120
Cronon, E. David, xviii, 92, 127
Cuba, 6, 84
    and the BSL, 87–88
Cuffee, Paul, 66

Davis, M. J., 76
Díaz, Porfirio, 56–57
Domingo, W. A., xiv, xvi
Douglass, Frederick, 18, 108
Du Bois, W.E.B., xvi, 12, 15–17,
  21–22, 30, 43–44, 94, 102,
  107–8
Dutch East India Company, 69
Dyer Anti-Lynching Bill, 103

El Centro, California, 115
Elaine, Arkansas, 24, 28–29
Elder Dempster, 67, 69–71
Ethiopia, 120
Ewing, Adam, 84

Farr, James, 54–56, 98, 107
Ferdinand, Franz, xx
Filipinos, xvii, 39, 46–47, 110, 115, 125
France, xx, 6, 12, 14, 21–22, 29, 30
Freedmen's Bureau, 4
Friends of Negro Freedom, 105

Gandhi, Mahatma, 75, 107
Garvey, Marcus
    and the BSL, 48, 65–68, 73–74, 80–89, 91–94, 127
    in California, 97–98
    Caribbean, 24–28, 52, 90
    death of, 121
    history of, xiii–xvi, 7–10, 13, 15–18
    and the Klan, 99–102, 107, 128
    and the NAACP, 108
    and the Negro World, 24, 52, 77, 81, 118, 124
    PCNA, 95–96, 98, 104–6, 109, 113, 128
    trial of, 92–93
    and the UNIA, 23, 42–45, 49, 66, 76, 113, 127–28
    and veterans, 30–32
Garveyism
    Africa, 72–73
    Black labor, 79
    Black Star Line, 65, 68
    in the Caribbean, 26–27, 35–37, 40–41, 44, 46, 52
    decline of, 129–30

Japanese interactions with, 48, 80–81
    in Mexico, 110
    rise of, xv, 3, 18–19, 23, 123–24
    in the West, xvii, xix, xxi, 32, 106–9, 112, 116–17, 121, 123, 128
Garvey's Watchman, xiii
General Goethals (Booker T. Washington), 88
Ghadar Party, 36, 51–53, 60, 117, 130
Gold Star Mothers, 82
Gordon, J. D., 43–45, 49, 61

Habitual Idlers Ordinance (1919), 27
Harlem, xiii–xvii, xix, 13, 15, 17–18, 48, 76, 87, 129
Harlem Hellfighters, 13
Harrison, Hubert, xiv, xvi, 15–16, 104
Haynes, Samuel, 27
Hayward, Colonel William, 13
Herero (Bantu ethnic group), 70
Hindu, 52, 54–56, 107
Hoover, J. Edgar, 31–32, 92

Imperial Daily Standard, 115
Imperial Wizard of the KKK, 101–2
India, xx, xxii, 50–56, 121, 125, 126
    discrimination of, 32, 50–52, 125, 130
    nationalism, xxi, xxii, xxiii, 33, 35, 50, 54, 63, 98,

107, 117
shipping, 74–76
Indigenous Americans, xvii, 7,
10–11, 32, 41, 68, 76, 111,
115

Jacques, Amy, xviii, 90
Jamaica, xiii–xiv, 6–7, 9, 24, 66,
79, 84, 88, 93
Japan, 9, 47–49, 53, 55, 66, 71
Japanese, xix, xxii, 20, 36, 51–52,
62–63, 77
Japanese nationalists, xxii, 33,
39–41, 55–56, 61, 81
sailors and dockworkers,
80–81
Jim Crow, 4, 7, 13, 15, 19, 32, 40,
76, 82–83, 124
Johnson, Reverend Daniel, 66
Jones, James Wormley, 31–32.
See also Agent 800

Kilroe, Edwin P., 86
Kimbangu, Simon, 72
Ku Klux Klan (KKK), xviii,
19–21, 36, 40–42, 60,
99–104, 106, 125, 127–28

La Nación, xiv, 8
Lagos Weekly Record, 73
Lewis, Rupert, xviii
Liberia, 43, 61, 67, 72, 84, 86,
92–94
Liberty Hall, 13
Little Liberia, 61
Los Angeles Evening Press, 43
Los Angeles UNIA division, xix,
43, 45, 77, 95–96

Los Angeles Urban League, 44
Lumbee Indigenous, 11

Macbeth, Hugh, Sr., 61
Madero, Francisco, 57
Manifest Destiny, 69
Martin, Tony, xviii, 84
The Messenger, 12, 16, 44, 104
Mexican Americans, xxii–xxiii,
10–11, 36, 40, 58–63
Mexican Revolution, 60, 62,
115
Miller, Loren, 119
Mohamed Ali, Dusé, 9
Morel, E. D., 71
Moton, R. R., 67
Mulzac, Hugh, 88

NAACP, xvi, 5, 15, 21, 30,
40, 42, 44, 92, 97–98, 100,
102–3, 108, 113, 119–20
Nama (African ethnic group),
70
National Negro Business
League, 42
National Negro Congress, 40
National Urban League, xvi, 40,
44
Negro World, 24, 28, 30, 39, 52,
72, 77, 81, 100, 118, 124
New Negro Movement, xvi, 25,
32, 42

Oakland, California, 37, 46,
79–80, 97–98, 109, 127
Office of Naval Intelligence, 54,
107
Oregon, xvii, 35, 37, 41, 52, 82,

99, 105
Owen, Chandler, 16, 44, 104–5

Pacific Basin, xvii, 121
Pacific Coast Hindustan
   Association (PCHA), 51
Pacific Coast Negro
   Improvement Association
   (PCNIA), 96, 98, 104–6,
   109
Padmore, George, 118, 120
Panama, 26, 37, 53, 75, 90
Panama Canal, 26, 80, 90
Paris Peace Conference, 47, 49,
   81, 121, 125
Pershing, General John J., 58
Plan de San Diego, 58
Plessy v. Ferguson, 4
Progressive Farmers and
   Household Union of
   America, 28
Pullman porters, 38–39
Pullman Company, 38

Randolph, A. Philip, xvi, 15, 16,
   44, 103
Reconstruction, 3–5, 10, 16, 19,
   32, 77, 102, 110
Red Summer (1919), 24, 42
Rega, Prince U. Kaba, 67

S.S. *Antonio Maceo*, 86
S.S. *China*, 85
S.S. *Frederick Douglass*, 86
S.S. *Kanawha*, 91
S.S. *Liberia*, 67
S.S. *Phyllis Wheatley*, 91–92
S.S. *Shadyside*, 91

S.S. *Yarmouth*, 86–89
Sam, Alfred Charles, 66
San Diego, California, 40, 42,
   59–60, 94, 109
San Francisco Chronicle, 52
Scottsboro Boys, 119–20
Seattle, Washington, 35, 37, 40,
   42, 45, 47, 52, 77–78, 80–81,
   94, 97, 109
sharecroppers, 28–30
Sierra Leone, 66, 72–73, 84, 92
Singh Bhakna, Sohan, 52, 117
Spanish-American War, 12

Tabernacle Baptist Church,
   43–44
Taylor, Quintard, 77–78
Thompson, Noah, 43–44, 95,
   105
Times of Nigeria, 74
Tolbert, Emory, xix, xxi, 44
Trinidad Workingmen's
   Association (TWA), 27
Trotter, William Monroe, 108
Tulsa Race Riots, 42, 90–91
Tuskegee Institute, xiv, 45, 67

United Fruit Company (UFC),
   6, 75–76, 90
United States Shipping Board
   (USSB), 85, 88
Universal Negro Improvement
   Association (UNIA), 3, 9,
   18, 25–29, 31–32, 48–49, 66,
   68, 70, 76, 84, 86–89, 91–92,
   100–102, 111, 113, 120–21,
   127
   in Africa, 72

establishment of, xiii–xvii,
13, 15, 23
in Los Angeles, xix, 42–45,
49, 77, 83, 90, 95–99,
104–6, 109, 128
and Mexican Americans,
60–62
in San Francisco, 49,
53–55, 79, 97–98, 107
in Seattle, 40, 81
Up from Slavery (Washington),
xiv, 9
Vandism, 72
Villa, Pancho, 57–58
Vincent, Theodore, xviii, 60

Walker, Madam C. J., xvi
Washington, Booker T., xiv–xv,
9, 15, 67, 102, 108, 112, 114
White Star Line, 65
Wilson, Woodrow, 6, 10, 20, 48,
58
Woermann-Linie Line, 69–71
Wooten, Charles, 24

X, Malcolm, xv, 15, 92

YMCA, 30, 42

Zimmermann Telegram, 57

ABOUT THE AUTHOR

Author photo by Joe O'Brien

Holly M. Roose is Promise Scholar program director and instructor at the University of California at Santa Barbara. The Promise Scholars program funds and supports nearly 500 low-income, first-generation, and underrepresented students in higher education at UCSB. Dr. Roose received her PhD in history with an emphasis in Black studies from UC Santa Barbara and her master's degree in African and African American studies from Columbia University. She has taught courses in Black Studies and history and currently teaches classes for struggling students on how to navigate the university. Her research focuses on transnational social movements, the global Black experience, and the impacts of Garveyism on global populations of color. She is from Huntsville, Alabama, and currently lives in Santa Barbara, California.

CPSIA information can be obtained
at www.ICGtesting.com
Printed in the USA
LVHW110010220322
713996LV00023B/626/J